HEALING EVERYWHERE

JOHN GAYNER BANKS, D.S.T.

Healing Everywhere

A Book of Healing Mission Talks

by

JOHN GAYNER BANKS, D.S.T.

Published by The International Order Of Saint Luke The Physician
Copyright, 1961
2nd Printing 1962
3rd Printing 1966
4th Printing 1974
5th Printing 1978
6th Printing 1980
7th Printing 1991
8th Printing, 2001

Healing Everywhere

John Gaynor Banks, D.S.T.

Based on the original publication (1951) as edited and updated in 2007 by order of the North American Board of Directors of the International Order of St. Luke the Physician.

Editing team:
Rev Don Crary, Vice-President of the Board;
Rev. Betty Luginbill Past President of the Board;
and Rev. Dr. Barbara Pursey, Director of Region 11.

Produced for the OSL by Stillpoint-by-the-Sea media.
Design/layout: Ann Pressly
Cover design: Linda Miller

ISBN 9781890498306
FOR ADDITIONAL COPIES: 1-800-675-9228
or www.orderofstluke.org. E-mail: oslresourcecenter@satx.rr.com

This 75th Anniversary Edition
is dedicated to the glory of God
and in memory of Backman Wong, Region 1.

The Directors of the OSL are grateful to all of the individuals whose donations helped pay for these reprintings of ***Healing Everywhere.***

FOREWORD

IN the 1930's the Rev. Dr. John Gaynor Banks along with his wife Ethel began a prayer group at St. Luke's Episcopal Church in San Diego, California the purpose of which was to respond more fully to the mandate of Jesus as stated in Luke 9:1-2 which was to tell people about the kingdom of God and to heal the sick. It was also a response to what he found lacking in the church of his day which was to take seriously Christ's mandate "to heal the sick." It became their goal to pray for the sick and to work at helping to restore the healing ministry of the Gospel to its rightful place in the teaching and practice of the Church. I suspect that neither would have dreamt of the far reaching influence that they would have had not only on their own denomination, but on churches of all denominations. It was due to the prayers and efforts of people like the Banks and others that the Church began to see its responsibility and to take seriously the mandate of Jesus "to heal the sick." "Healing Everywhere" is a collection of Dr. Banks' lectures and mission talks given at missions held all over the United States and Canada, in which he presents the fundamental Gospel teaching on the healing ministry of Jesus. In this book he addresses the issues of how people can experience God's healing touch in their own lives as well as how they can take Jesus' mandate seriously and become ministers of Christian healing helping others to experience in their lives that same touch of God's healing love.

When the Board of Directors of the Order of Saint Luke looked at "Healing Everywhere" we saw that its message was timeless and its teaching was universal and relevant for every age but we also realized that the format and some of the language and concepts needed to be changed and updated to express these universal truths in ways that would be more meaningful for people of our day. It was our hope that the richness of its message and teaching could be of benefit to Christians of today just as it was to Christians in Banks' day. What we have tried to do with this new edition is to make those appropriate changes but in so doing to preserve the style of the writer and the essence of his message.

Being a priest of the Episcopal Church of the United States, much of the teaching and theology of John Gaynor Banks comes from his Anglican background which sometimes raises the question "Is the Order of Saint Luke a ministry under the umbrella of the Episcopal or Anglican Church?" The answer is no, the Order is totally separate and independent from all denominational jurisdictions but benefits and is enriched by the traditions of all the churches that now make up its ecumenical nature.

The legacy of John Gaynor Banks in writing "Healing Everywhere" is that it not only provides a foundation for the teaching and practice of the healing ministry of Jesus in the Church but is also the basis for the world wide ministry of the International Order of Saint Luke the Physician which is now active in countries all around the world. Members of the Order are still working under the same mandate and with the same purpose which is to be ministers of God's healing love and to be leaven in helping the Church return the healing ministry to its rightful place in its practice and presentation of the Gospel message.

Thanks to the Holy Spirit working through such organizations as the Order of Saint Luke, healing services and the ministry of healing is becoming a common feature of the work and witness in many churches. In order to respond to the growing need to develop healing ministries in congregations the Order of Saint Luke is working to expand its ministry to include teaching and training. It is our hope that we can help clergy and the members of congregations to become ministers of healing and to assist them in the developing and training of healing ministry teams to work within the context of the local parish situation.

I believe that the teaching in "Healing Everywhere" not only continues to provide a foundation for the healing ministry in churches but is as relevant today as it was when it was first presented. I commend this new edition to you for reading, study and reflection and may you find in it new insights and a renewed inspiration to take the mandate of your baptism seriously to be tellers of the good news and healers of the sick.

Lawrence William Mitchell
North American Director

If you would like further information about the Order of Saint Luke and how you might become a part of this world wide ministry please contact our North American Office in San Antonio, Texas.

P.O. Box 780909, San Antonio, Texas, 78278-0909
Toll Free Number in all of North America:
(877) 992-5222
E-Mail: OSL2@satx.rr.com
Web Site: www.orderofst.luke.org

CONTENTS

INTRODUCTION

THIS BOOK is an attempt to reproduce in readable style all the best features of a mission of Christian healing as conducted in numerous places throughout the United States and Canada under the auspices of The Fellowship of Saint Luke and The Order of Saint Luke. The author makes no attempt to eliminate the spontaneous note of these mission talks. On the contrary he feels the book will serve its purpose by preserving the conversational style and unconventional phraseology which characterize mission addresses.

The topics vary at these missions, but there is a certain normal sequence which the missioner has found valuable, almost unavoidable, if the whole truth about healing is to be presented in five or six days.

Just because the active ministry of healing is still a novelty in many churches, it has been found desirable to mention the practice of the early Church, to which all modern churches look for authority and precedents. And because the people who attend a mission of healing come far more for help than for instruction, we emphasize early in the week the need for conversion (or a fresh experience of God in Christ) and the close connection between forgiveness of sin and healing of sickness. While we recognize that there is a basic theology which treats of confession and absolution as long-established practices of the Church

Universal, the effort made in these missions is rather to simplify the process for the average seeker, stressing the simple scriptural approach rather than any particular liturgical practice or private and sacramental ministry.

In this book, as in the mission services held locally, I have tried to make the way as clear as possible for the seeker. The teaching side of this ministry must be quickly supplemented by practical advice. The seeker wants to know "How to do it" – and we try to meet this demand. We find that the large majority of seekers fail in their quest for very simple reasons. One is a lack of a true conversion. We use the word pretty much in the light of William James' famous definition: "Conversion is that process, gradual or sudden, whereby a soul previously divided, and consciously wrong, inferior and unhappy, becomes unified, and consciously right, superior and happy." After reading the chapter on conversion, readers should be able to kneel down (wherever they may be) and offer themselves afresh to God, believing that God himself will perform the "converting" process. The same applies largely to the chapter on forgiveness. A few readers may be able to avail themselves of the help of a confessor or counselor, to whom they can unburden their souls. But the majority of readers will need to get quiet and alone and pour out their souls to God in the silence. I am sure there is a species of absolution which comes to such souls when they have paid the price; and it is an important step toward healing, whether of soul or body. The same applies largely to the chapter on the cure of fear and anxiety. Such a large proportion of seekers are kept from their much-needed healing because fear inhibits them, usually some particular fear, though not always clearly defined in the consciousness of the seeker. It is a simple expedient, after a season of meditation and reflection, to write down one's fears on paper and then offer them to God, with the final ritual of burning the paper and deliberately relinquishing the fear. In some cases this ritual may be performed more than once, though it is obviously more satisfactory to do it in such fashion that no repetition is needed.

The technique of dedication comes also near the beginning of a mission because it clears the way for healing. This subject deserves long and careful treatment and could become an act of worship, bringing holy joy and inward satisfactions. But in this particular sequence it is presented as a preparation for healing, just because we find so often that the body itself (or some part of the body) presents obstacles and hence requires careful attention leading to a fresh commitment, as shown in the chapter on this subject.

On the part of those who read this book with special hopes of deriving healing power for themselves (or on behalf of those near and dear to them) we ask patience in this matter of reading. "Faith comes from what is heard, and what is heard comes through the Word of Christ." (Romans 10:17). Your reading of this book must take the place of actually listening to the spoken word. You will find great benefit in reading the book prayerfully and attentively several times, especially those chapters which touch a responsive chord in your own soul. "The unfolding of your words gives light." (Psalms 119:130). A receptive, non-argumentative attitude in reading this book will yield rich dividends.

Four people have worked hard in the production of this book. Their efforts have been consistently to recreate the atmosphere of a healing mission, so far as that is possible on paper. So we beg you to "tune in" as these "recordings" are played simultaneously before your eyes and your ears! "The Word is near you, on your lips and in your heart" (that is, the word of faith that we proclaim); because if you confess with your lips that Jesus is Lord, and believe in your heart that God raised him from the dead, you will be saved." (Romans 10:8-9). To "be saved" means literally to be made whole. Let us ponder this larger meaning of "salvation."

It will be pretty obvious to most of our readers that these chapters are (with few exceptions) tape recordings of lectures actually given by the author at recent missions of healing. These recordings have been edited only to eliminate some irrelevant material and to avoid repetitions unavoidable in such talks. In the chapters based on the healing ministry of Jesus as recorded in the four gospels, the missioner deliberately used the fourth dimensional style of speaking. By this is meant an attempt to rise above limitations of time this ministry of healing as offered in a mission such as here recorded.

Readers may welcome this fragment from the Middle Ages as making the way to the living Jesus more accessible. It is related that Richard Hooker, a famous Elizabethan divine, was asked by the Queen for his opinion as to whether the doctrine of the Real Presence should be generally affirmed by the Church. "Is our Lord actually present on the Altar in the consecrated elements?" asked the Queen. Richard Hooker took but a few moments to answer the question, which came back to the Queen in the following words –

" His was the Word that spake it,
He took the bread and brake it,
And what His Word doth make it,
That I believe and take it!"

Healing faith is very much like this. We sense his presence in our healing service with childlike faith. We come because he invites us. We read his definite promises of healing. We claim these promises, by ourselves or in the presence of friends and helpers. The "signs" follow. (See Mark 16:17). What practical results may we expect? That depends upon each individual seeker. "According to your faith let it be done to you." (Matthew 9:29).

James Moore Hickson, an English healer who visited America 45 years ago, used to tell his audiences: "God will meet you where you are and he will give you all that you are able to receive!" This book will help you to receive more!

The electrical recordings on which this book is based were made by Mr. Charles W. Hoefle, OSL, of Oklahoma City, Oklahoma, and Mr. Ralph Keehn, OSL, and Mr. Harold Keehn, OSL, of Seguin, Texas.

The transcribing was done largely by Mrs. Royal J. Gibson, OSL, of Oklahoma City, Oklahoma, assisted by the Keehn brothers. To all of these good friends in the OSL I am deeply grateful, for without their assistance this book would not be now available.

Please join me in prayer that this book may bring strength, healing and consolation to every reader.

Your brother in Christ,
JOHN GAYNER BANKS,
Warden Emeritus OSL

QUESTIONS

1. What do you still find to be true in the Church today that Banks mentions as being true in 1961?
2. What ideas does the author express about conversion and forgiveness?
3. What suggestion is made to relieve a person of fear and anxiety?
4. What are some approaches to helping people accept healing in the church?

STUDY

LEARN

ABSORB

BELIEVE

AND FOLLOW JESUS CHRIST

I

PRAYER AND HEALING IN THE EARLY CHURCH

PRAYER is the secret of every successful healing mission. But not just any kind of prayer! When you have learned to pray the right way, you will have taken a long step in the direction of healing for yourself and for those you're praying for.

What is the Right Kind of Prayer?

I am a student of words. Words are full of power and fascination for me. An ordinary, mediocre term will sometimes pop up and blossom out with new meaning. I recommend to you the study of words if you would have God speak to you day by day. The Word of God is a beautiful and flexible phrase. This word may come to you in the most ordinary way. Some word that you have been using for years may come to you with fresh meaning as you read this book, and it may prove a Word of God for you at this time.

Think for just a moment about the word "prayer." Ask anyone, "What do you mean by prayer?"

"Prayer? Oh, prayer is asking God for something!"

Is it? No! But unfortunately that is a popular idea of prayer. To pray to God is to beg God to give you something – so many people think. That is part of the meaning of prayer, of course, but it is not the most important part by any means. We need a larger and richer concept if we are to pray effectively for healing. So let us look at some of the Bible words for prayer.

You would be amazed if you could read these Bible terms for prayer in the original languages. They are translated by the one word "prayer" in the King James Version of the Bible. But let us see what the original word meant.

In the Old Testament you will find many times in the original Hebrew the word *palal* which has been translated "prayer." What does *palal* mean? It does not mean prayer in our sense. It means to pray in joyous astonishment. Watch the faces of average churchgoers in the middle of an average eleven o'clock service on Sunday morning. Are they praising God in joyous astonishment? I wonder!

There is another remarkable word used many times for "prayer" in the Old Testament. It is the word *tephillah*, and it means to marvel at the wonders of

God and of your own soul. That is a very broad translation, but that is the idea. Suppose we could pray like that! Wouldn't it be marvelous and thrilling? Wouldn't it put new life into us to have that concept of prayer translated into practice?

Then, the New Testament has its own words for prayer. There is the Greek word *euche* which appears frequently in the Gospels. *Euche* means to desire fervently. There is another word, *aiteo*, which is very close to it. It means to yearn after, to want a thing tremendously with all your heart. This is what the New Testament means by prayer.

Now, it is part of the procedure of a healing ministry to recapture something of the glow, the power, the significance of those old Bible words. Let us learn to find something in God that will fill us with astonishment at the wonder of him and of our own souls find something that will enable you to praise him in joyous expectation. That is faith. Faith is joyous expectation! "By prayer… with thanksgiving, let your requests be made known to God." (Philippians 4:6). But let there be a great wealth of desire back of it and, believe me, your prayers shall not be disappointed. God will prove himself if you will let him. Let us seek a new experience of prayer as we read this book. Come to God, thanking him for what he is, thanking him for his magnificent promises, and expecting wonderful things from him! William Carey, a pioneer missionary of India, once said, "Attempt great things for God and expect great things from God." This is the right kind of prayer.

But What is Our Authority for This Message of Healing?

The quickest way to get it is by turning to the ninth chapter of the Gospel of Luke and reading the opening verses, then turning to the tenth chapter of the same book and reading the opening verses. From there, go over to the first three chapters of the Acts of The Apostles to get a true perception of this whole work.

Now, what do you find in the ninth chapter of the Gospel of Luke? There you have the story of the sending out of twelve men. These twelve are now known by the name of "apostles." In some churches you will find statues of them, or you will see stained glass windows of them with halos around their heads, looking very other-worldly. But they were typical men of their age, the type that Jesus mingled with day by day, men that he selected as agents for the spreading of his message.

First, he called them together. This was a corporate assignment. There is no individualism here. Jesus did not send one man out to carry on his message alone. He trained the twelve in fellowship and then sent them out with a wonderful commission. He gave them power. Power means enablement. He gave them authority. Authority charged them with confidence. They knew they were authorized to give this message. They were co-creators with God of a new age.

Now, what was the scope of their commission? Jesus was very definite: he gave them power over all demons and to cure diseases. He sent them out to preach the kingdom of God and to heal. "Ah," someone says, "but you've been talking about the twelve apostles. Naturally, Peter, James and John and all the others would be able to do these things. They were picked men. They were highly gifted. They could do it, but don't expect us to do anything like that today!" If that is the way you feel, turn over to chapter ten.

Here we find seventy, not twelve! And they are not apostles. They are just ordinary disciples – what we would call "laity" today. What is the commission given them? It is very much like the other. They are to go out two-by-two. No lone wolfing! "Whenever you enter a town and they do welcome you... cure the sick who are there, and say to them, 'The kingdom of God has come near to you.'" (Luke 10:8-9). Isn't that pretty much what he said to the others? But someone says, "Jesus gave that power to the seventy to start this new movement on its way, but we have no right to claim these powers for ourselves today." That certainly is not a logical deduction from the data that you have in your New Testament. Jesus repeatedly instructed those whom he sent out to preach, teach and heal. The Church accepts the obligation to preach and teach. If we are preaching the Gospel and teaching the things that Jesus has committed to us, is there any authority for ignoring the third category? The three – preaching, teaching and healing – go together. They are not to be practiced separately. Healing is a part of the total evangelistic obligation of the Church. These three go clear back to the apostles. How much of the original gospel are we giving to people today? Are we building up our churches as a result of that larger evangel which Jesus commissioned us to proclaim? I covet the time when healing will be part of the program of every Christian Church, no matter what its name is.

So I go back to the early Church and I see that Jesus commissioned his followers to teach, preach and to heal, and he gave them authority and power over all demons and to cure all diseases. There is nothing of the parable in this, nothing mysterious, nothing mystical. They were utterly committed to a program of loyalty to Jesus and the carrying out of the gospel that he had proclaimed to them. When we preach the gospel but fail to include the power to heal that Jesus emphasized, we miss the rich results that would come through total obedience.

To preach the kingdom of God is to affirm the presence of God. God is here in our very midst. Our task is to announce the immediate presence of God. That is the condition under which healing can be done. When people suddenly become aware of the wholly other, that wonderful, awe-inspiring presence of God, then it is that they get down on their knees and ask God for those great gifts that he is ready to give. Healing is part of it. Healing is inevitable when the kingdom of God is truly affirmed. This is the real meaning of "Your kingdom come. Your will be done on earth, as it is in heaven." (Matthew 6:10).

The story is told of a Franciscan monk, a young man in Texas, who got the reputation for great power in prayer – so much so that people attributed to him the working of miracles. He made no such claim himself, but the people around said, "Father works miracles through his prayers." And so it seemed. Mothers would bring their children to him and he would pray for them and they would recover. Business men brought problems to him and he would pray and their fears would leave. Children loved him and he played with them and blessed them. It seemed as though he had a prayer for every sort of human need. And his fame spread. People came from a hundred miles around to have this Franciscan monk pray for them. And finally the head of his order, the Superior, sent for him. He said, "Father, I hear you've been working miracles in your parish."

"No, sir, no indeed! You must have got an exaggerated report. I'm not working any miracles."

"But I get these reports, not from one or two, but from many people," said his superior. "Tell me, how do you do it? How do you work these miracles?"

And the young man said, "I don't work any miracles, Father!"

"Well, explain yourself. What is the secret of your reputation and this great thing that you're doing?"

Then, reluctantly the young monk said, "Well, Father, a hundred times every morning and a hundred times every night I pray, 'Thy will be done on earth as it is done in heaven.' That is all."

Have you ever thought of what might happen if we really learned to pray that prayer? If we really expected God's perfect will to be done on earth in us, today, in our own towns, in our own homes, under our own conditions – God's perfect will to be done on earth as it is done in heaven? Yet surely this prayer lies at the heart of the gospel.

It is these little words like "gospel" that fool us. What is the meaning of the word "gospel"? Gospel comes from two old Saxon words, "God's spell." The spell of God. You put God's spell on a person and that breaks the force of evil in that person. Take the word "wicked." Look up its derivation. It is derived from the old English word "bewitched." A wicked person is a bewitched person. What do you do with a bewitched person? You have to break the spell! And you break the spell by putting God's spell upon him. The gospel is the simple expedient of breaking the spell of evil in any life. You break the evil spell by God's spell, or the gospel. And it really works! Say to them, "The kingdom of God or the kingdom of heaven has come near to you."

Well, what results followed the carrying out of Jesus' commission? We don't have much report about the twelve. We know they did wonderful things. We know they witnessed honestly, courageously and conspicuously in some cases. But we have a very quick report about the seventy. Read it for yourself in chapter ten of the Gospel of Luke: "The seventy returned with joy saying, 'Lord, in your name, even the demons submit to us!'" (Luke 10:17). Did Jesus rebuke them? He did not! Did he tell them to be very, very cautious with this new power? He did not! He rejoiced with them. He said, "See, I have given you authority ...over all the power of the enemy: and nothing will hurt you." (Luke 10:19). If we would take these actual words of Jesus and recapture something of the glamour, the glow of that early scene, I think all our fears and anxieties and apprehensions would vanish into thin air.

Then Jesus turned his eyes upward. He had recognized the returning ones. He had given them one little warning: do not rejoice too much that the demons are subject unto you, but rather rejoice that your names are written in heaven. (See Luke 10:20). We know a little of what that means today. We must get rid of any personal prestige or glory in this. We are ministers; we are servants; we are commissioned to do a job. That job is the work of Jesus himself. We are accessories to his will. And *his name*, when we use his name, will be the authority and the only authority we need. Jesus looks up to heaven and he talks with God about all this in a most beautiful colloquy. "I thank you, Father, Lord of heaven and earth, because you have hidden these things from the wise and intelligent, and have revealed them to infants; yes, Father, for such was your gracious will." (Luke 10:21). We shall have more to say about this later. But are you among the "infants"? Are you satisfied to be among the infants? The infants were the initiated ones. The word in Sanskrit for "infants" can mean "initiate." It means those who are entering into a new kind of life. They are infants on the new plane of being. They are infants, but they are infants in a new experience of life. And in that new experience of life, all these wonderful things can happen and do happen.

The Apostle Luke is a master artist in the way he depicts these things. He is constantly painting word-pictures for us. He had an inspired imagination that captured the very essence of truth. He tells us that Jesus looked back to the disciples (after he had addressed the Father) and said to them, "Blessed are the eyes that see what you see! For I tell you that many prophets and kings desired to see what you see, but did not see them; and to hear what you hear, but did not hear them." (Luke 10:23-24). Think about that and ask yourself in the presence of God, "To what extent are my eyes really open to this fuller revelation? To what extent are my ears alert to the truth of God that is coming at this time?" "See, I have given you power! ... Jesus rejoiced in the Holy Spirit!" (Luke 10:19, 21). Moffatt's translation says, "He [Jesus] thrilled with joy ... saying, 'I praise thee, Father, Lord of heaven and earth, for concealing this from the wise and learned and revealing it to the simple-minded [babes].' (Luke 10:21 - Moffatt).[1]

How was that healing ministry perpetuated?

The Apostle Luke wrote two books: one is called the Gospel of Luke and the other is called the Acts of

---

[1] From The Bible – A New Translation, by James Moffatt. Copyright 1922 - 1935 and 1950 by Harper & Brothers. Used by permission.

the Apostles. The Gospel of Luke deals chiefly with the work of Jesus and his teachings. The Acts of the Apostles deals with the perpetuation of the gospel through the Church. I use the word "church" in its largest possible connotation.

Now, how was this commission perpetuated? You will find the essence of it in the first three chapters of the Acts. The first three chapters of the Acts are important for the reason that they show how all the teachings of Jesus were carried on by his body, the Church.

The third chapter of the Acts introduces us to the healing as practiced by the apostles. I am using the word apostles here in the large sense, including disciples who were not among the twelve. When we talk about the Apostolic Church, we mean the church of the first centuries. Who were those first Christians? What did they do? How did they work? What did they say? What results did they produce? What contributions do they have to make to this age in which we live? Read the Acts of the Apostles. Read carefully! Read between the lines! Use your imagination! You will be surprised at how much you will get out of those first three chapters alone. Chapter three, then, records the first healing miracle in the Christian Church after Jesus had ascended into heaven. It is an amazing story, a long story. It is the longest record of a healing miracle in the Bible. It occupies part of chapter four as well.

When you read this miracle thoughtfully, you will rub your eyes and say, "Can this be true? Did this really happen?" Yes, you know it did! You can't explain it, but you know it happened. But how did it happen? That is what we want to know and if we want to know enough, if we have enough eager desire in prayer, we shall certainly find the answer.

The miracle in chapter three is adequately explained by something which is recorded in chapter two. The clue to chapter three is in chapter two. And what does chapter two tell us? It is the story of Pentecost. If you want the power in chapter three, you have to have an experience of Pentecost as reflected in chapter two. You know that marvelous chapter. They were all together with one accord – praying! And then, the Holy Spirit was poured out on them in great power, and from that outpouring at Pentecost came the sermon of Peter. And out of the sermon of Peter came the conversion of three thousand souls. And out of that initial revival we get the little early Church (summarized into about seven verses at the end of chapter two). "They devoted themselves to the apostles' teaching and fellowship, to the breaking of bread, and the prayers." (Acts 2:42). There is your original ecumenical church in the forty-second verse of the second chapter of the Acts. That explains the power that healed the lame man in chapter three.

Some of you are interested and say, "'That is wonderful, but how in the world do you get the miracle of Pentecost? That too is a miracle!" Look back a little further – in chapter one – and there you will find the explanation of chapter two. Pray tell us what is this wonderful thing in chapter one? Why it is the prayer group! It is the first Christian prayer group! Will I dare risk the criticism that comes from saying what follows? Chapter one contains the story of the first Novena! That is actually true. The first Novena was the work of the prayer group in the first chapter of the Acts of the Apostles.

What is a Novena? A novena is a prayer continued for nine days for a specific intention. There is wonderful power in Novenas. Don't you doubt it. It can be abused! Certainly it can! It can be surrounded with superstition! Yes, indeed! But there is a value, a real power, in a Novena. The Novena, the prayer for one thing continued over a period of nine days, was first held (as devout Catholics will tell you – but they don't have a monopoly on Novenas) by one hundred and twenty Christians in the upper room at Jerusalem as recorded in the first chapter of the Acts of the Apostles.

Now, I'm not silly enough to imagine that the mere mechanical repetition of a prayer for nine days is going to bring about miracles, but I know enough psychology to know that anything that you hold tenaciously for nine days without wavering is very likely to come into expression. And there is perfectly sound psychology back of the Catholic Novena. My eyes were opened to this about four years ago. I was on my way back from a group of Missions in the East, and I stopped for two days in Denver to visit an old friend of mine who is rector of the Epiphany Church. Epiphany Church is a very unique church, not like any other church in the United States. It is an Episcopal church, but it has ideas of its own. And every November they have a Novena. It is a Novena for healing, and they start it on the first day of November and it is continued for nine days. You put your name in the box in the vestibule of the church and you put your special intention on paper and you light a candle! These little red votive lights burn along one whole side of the church for the whole nine days.

"Well," I said to the rector, "Now, do you mean that these people really get answers to their prayers?"

"Do they get answers to their prayers?" he replied. "Do you think they would come here for nine days if they didn't?" Then he told me the most amazing stories about the answers to prayers that they get at this Novena each year. Hundreds of answers to prayer! I went there and preached the opening sermon for this Novena. It is the only time I've ever taken part in a Novena. It was on a Tuesday morning at ten o'clock, a most uninteresting time of the week. Yet there were two hundred and sixty people in that church to start their Novena on the first of November. I mention this for only one reason. We need more perseverance in our prayers! There is a place for a Novena. It carries out the idea of persevering prayer. It is the Apostle Paul's meaning when he says, "Pray without ceasing." (I Thessalonians 5:17). It is taking God at his word. You can discount anything that seems superstitious or irrational – just forget it! But there is power, POWER in a prayer continued, Continued, CONTINUED!

Let me tell you a story which illustrates the point. I was writing out a new study course last year. I wanted to find something about the work of healing in the early Church. There is not a great deal written about that, but there is some valuable data, and in one of these old books (a book written by a very scholarly Englishman from Oxford), I found this little story. It made me smile and yet it taught me a good lesson.

There was a young girl in the second century who had a growth in her neck. She went to the priest and said, "Father, pray for me that I may be healed." The priest did what was quite common at that time. He went and got the holy oil, and he anointed this girl on her neck for the cure of this growth. And nothing happened! She was very disappointed and the priest was disappointed, but he thought there must be something blocking the way. When she came back the next day, the girl said, "Father, the growth is still here."

"All right, my daughter," he replied, "I'll anoint you again." He anointed her the second time. Still nothing happened!

The third day she came back again. "Still there!"

"All right," he said, "I'll anoint you again." He anointed her again, prayed over her, gave her a blessing, sent her away, and she did not come for a day or two. But a few days later, she came back again. The growth was still there.

This time the priest was angry, not with the girl, but with the force of evil that held her in bondage. And in a gesture of righteous indignation, he took the little vial and poured the holy oil down her throat and made her swallow it. And immediately the growth vanished! She was cured.[2]

Now, do not think that was just magic. And, please, do not think I would do anything, so erratic in a mission today, but I learned a lesson from this story. First, I learned the lesson of perseverance. The priest was not put off because nothing happened the first time. Nor was the girl. She came back. She came back four or five times. Also, the priest was willing to change his technique. He didn't think that the mere mechanical repetition of any one method was going to bring about results. Then, while he was not angry with the girl, he was filled with righteous

---

[2] Told by Father Fuller, S. S. J. E., in his book on Anointing.

indignation against the powers of evil which held her in bondage. Jesus, in one place, spoke of the forces of evil which held a woman in bondage and he released her.

There is a great value in perseverance. There is something to be learned from the Novena – that continuation of prayer and the spirit of prayer and that righteous indignation against anything that interferes with the perfect will of God. So let us not be weary in well-doing. Let us learn to fulfill the conditions for healing. Read the first three chapters of the Acts of the Apostles. Read in a number of different translations – Weymouth, Moffatt, Twentieth Century, the Bible in Modern English, the Revised Standard Version as well as the King James. They are all translations.

God is no respecter of persons, but he is a respecter of conditions, and when we make the conditions right at our end, God will do the work at his end. If God's maximum blessings for you are not coming to expression in your body, in your soul, in your circumstances, it is because conditions are not right. Prayer, thought, communion and fellowship will help to dissolve adverse conditions that hinder and thwart the perfect will of God. It took the first Christians nine days together to adjust matters, to get right with each other – perhaps as well as with God. But when they were right, then the power came though with pentecostal force and amazing miracles happened. The spirit of God is able to produce fellowship, *koinonia* (the Greek word for fellowship) – real, deep oneness. When that oneness is present in our prayers, in our fellowship, in our intercessions, in our healing work, then God's miracles are inevitable. You can't stop them. When the conditions are right, then God can work and then God will work. "The Lord worked with them ... by the signs that accompanied (the message)." (Mark 16:20).

Spiritual healing comes "through ... the faith which is through Jesus." (Acts 3:16). That is, Christ is the great healer, and the Holy Spirit is "the lord and giver of life." Not until we consider the true source from which all life and healing come, can we pray intelligently for the full restoration of this ministry. Not until we realize that the Christ nature, which is imparted to us, is the true source of all increase of life, can we interpret as we ought the simple but powerful formula, "Preserve your body and soul to everlasting life."

Some years ago Bishop Manning of New York concluded a sermon with these words. "Our faith is in one who does not change, one whose love and power are still able to cleanse the sinner and heal the sick, and give life from above to all who will follow him; One in whom we can wholly trust for this life and for all eternity, Jesus Christ, the same yesterday, today and forever. "

Let us pray: Father in Heaven, we thank you for the ministry of Jesus and his disciples. We would like to join that band of disciples today. We would like to become members of his clinic. We would like to learn from him about this wonderful work of prayer in its manifold expressions. Take from our minds the strain and stress and let our ordered lives confess the beauty of your peace. Prepare us for blessing and power. Give us the secret of true healing and make us worthy successors of that first band of disciples who eventually conquered in your name. Bless this book and make it productive of results in my life and in the lives of all who read it, for the kingdom, and the power, and the glory are yours forever and ever. Amen.

Questions

1. What are the different meanings of prayer in the Hebrew (OT) and the Greek (NT)?
2. What suggestions are made for prayer?
3. In what ways are Bank's suggestions similar to MacNutt's "soaking prayer"?

II

CONVERSION AND HEALING

THE healing that I believe in would be utterly out of place, a liability rather than an asset, unless it could be integrated with the essential truth of the Christian faith and the practice of the Church itself. I am not here, and I do not wish to go anywhere with a divisive message. The Christian message that I seek, that has come to me rather slowly over a period of more than thirty years, is integral to the Christian faith. It is fundamental to the Christian faith, not something added later, rather something restored from a former age.

The summer of 1950 I spent on my thirteenth pilgrimage to England. I make these pilgrimages not just to visit friends or for vacational purposes, but to refresh my mind and to learn what is available in this particular area of Christian teaching and practice. Great Britain has been rather innovative in the field of spiritual therapy, somewhat ahead of other nations. We have one or two societies in this country among the orthodox churches practicing and teaching Christian healing; but they have six or seven in Britain, each one doing a fine work, producing its own literature, conducting its own conferences and doing all this very quietly and circumspectly.

Great Britain has what is called The Churches' Council of Healing, a very remarkable movement, carried on so quietly that very little is said in the press about it. It was started by Archbishop Temple of Canterbury. Archbishop Temple, like the good statesman he was, saw the futility of promoting Christian healing – healing by faith and prayer and sacraments – in his own Church alone. So at the very beginning he called together a group of leaders from the various churches: Church of England (Anglican), Presbyterian, Methodist, Baptist, and even one or two Quakers who were already very interested in healing. He organized them into what was called The Churches' Council of Healing. I attended, by invitation, their summer conference, which lasted three or four days. The talk I remember most was one on "The Healing Power of Christian Worship," given by Dr. J. Crowlesmith, pastor of the leading Methodist Church in Cambridge. He is the Chairman of the Commission on Healing of the English Methodist Church. Among other things, he said, "Healing services are very valuable and doubtless can bring tremendous help to people in distress and even facing despair. But have you ever thought of the therapeutic value of the ordinary Sunday morning service at eleven o'clock?" He explained to us what valuable, health-giving influence was to be found in a well-conducted Sunday morning service. He emphasized the "well-conducted." It must have a right balance of music, prayer, instruction and inspiration, and he said, "When you go to that kind of service, you will derive wonderful help even to the breaking down of disease and the building up of vital resistance, which, of course, is essentially a health enterprise."

Later in the summer, Dr. Crowlesmith presided over a meeting, convened largely, I think, by the Methodist Church in Cambridge, in which three days were spent in showing how the religion of Jesus Christ is the answer to the guilt complex that the psychologists and psychiatrists are always talking about. I am not a psychiatrist, but I have done a lot of research in psychology, and I know what a fearful thing that guilt complex is. Of course, there is sin back of it, usually, but the psychiatrist mustn't call it sin. There is no place for sin in psychiatry. That's an unprofessional word. We clergy can use that, but the psychiatrist calls it guilt, and if it gets to a chronic state and begins to disturb the mental and emotional balance, then it becomes a guilt complex. There are various kinds of guilt complexes. They spent three days working out this thing and showing how the Christian faith, the Christian religion, the gospel of Jesus Christ, has the final answer to the guilt complex. To me that was a marvelous piece of work, and much more important than the ordinary conference where they merely skim the surface and make beautiful platitudes about the power of faith to heal the sick.

In a healing mission it is necessary not only to listen to the message, but to also cooperate with the missioner. Spiritual therapy is a part of the work of any active prayer group. A healing mission is not all talking. It is working together in prayer. Group therapy is an enhanced activity of a real prayer group, functioning as a channel of God's healing power for those to whom they minister. A missioner is not a healer, but he has learned from years of experience how to pray for healing, and it is much easier to do that work of prayer when there are a number of people cooperating, putting themselves in a position for God to use them and to create centers, focal centers, through which the power of prayer may go forth and help and bless and heal those who are in such great need.

It ought to be made clear at the beginning of any book on Christian healing that there is a close relationship between healing and conversion. I refer here to the old-fashioned conversion which changes our lives, sometimes overnight, sometimes by a slower process. In this matter of conversion and healing we find two quite different lines which converge until they meet or blend in the complete wholeness of the seeker.

There is the strictly religious conversion where someone who doesn't know God at all (or who has perhaps "fallen from grace") is suddenly aroused to a sense of God's immediacy, and in that sense of divine immediacy gets down on their knees and offers their life spontaneously to God. They may do that from an impulse, a sort of irresistible compulsion from within. They may do it through listening to a sermon on the cross. Their eyes may suddenly be opened to the blood of Jesus Christ cleansing them from all sin! They may (or may not) get a tremendous conviction of sin. They usually pass through the stages of contrition, repentance and amendment. Please do not insist that everybody have the same experience! Do not assume that everybody must have a conversion experience just the way you got yours.

Definition of Conversion

Conversion may be variously defined. You may postulate a strictly religious conversion, or you may describe a strictly psychological conversion. May I cite a definition of conversion which might include both?

In his famous Gifford Lectures delivered in Scotland many years ago, William James of Harvard University presented his ***Varieties of Religious Experience*** (still available in the Modern Library series) and in that book he gives us this definition of conversion: "Conversion is that process, gradual or sudden, by which a soul, previously divided and consciously wrong, inferior and unhappy, becomes unified and consciously right, superior and happy." It is a classic definition and I accept it. It fits the conversion of Saul of Tarsus (see Acts, chapter nine) and it fits most ancient and modern stories of religious conversion. This definition also fits the experience described as "conversion" by clinical psychologists, though the human conditions here are quite different.

How Saul Became Paul

What was the experience of Saul of Tarsus? He was a scholar, a religious man, in the strictly orthodox sense, and a Hebrew born of Hebrews. He belonged to the sect of the Pharisees. He sat at the feet of Gamaliel. He was an intellectual, a philosopher, a theologian. And yet, on the inside, he was "wrong, inferior and unhappy." What was the secret? The answer is – he was divided! If you wish to pursue this aspect of the subject I refer you again to William James' book where you will find not only lectures on conversion, but also lectures on the sick soul and the divided soul and the process of its unification.

But you don't really require William James. The Apostle Paul gives in retrospect his own story with illuminating comments, written in the subsequent light of a marvelous experience. The diagnosis of his pathological condition is given eloquently in the seventh chapter of Romans, and chapter eight describes the process of his release, with supplementary comments in other epistles. The astute student should also read the three different accounts of his conversion given in the Acts of the Apostles – see chapters nine, twenty-two and twenty-six. You may be surprised to find your own religious experience accurately reflected in that of this great apostle! "For I do not do the good I want, but the evil that I do not want is what I do. When I want to do what is good, evil lies close at hand. For I delight in the law of God in my inmost self, but I see in my members another law at war with my mind, making me captive to the law of sin… Wretched man that I am! Who will rescue me from this body of this death?" (Romans 7:19-25). That is the cry of a man who is divided, who is "consciously wrong, inferior and unhappy." He had already developed some of the symptoms of schizophrenia; he was emotionally unstable; he was subject to fits of ungovernable rage. His persecutions of early Christians formed an outlet for this rage but gave him no enduring release. Dr.

Patterson-Smyth says he showed clear tendencies of a sadistic nature, that he flogged men and women for the perverse satisfaction it gave him. You see here to what lengths a man may go when he is "consciously wrong, inferior and unhappy!" He develops an inferiority complex that creates its own "window dressing" so that he appears to be just the opposite of who he really is. His persecution "compensates" for his own basic sense of inferiority. So the false sense of power, the power that culminates in cruelty, is a very familiar symptom to the modern psychologist. It can be treated psychologically, but it is a slow, painful job. And it doesn't always succeed. But there is a quicker way, if you have the courage; it is the way taken by Saul of Tarsus, challenged by that one who met him on the Damascus road! A supernatural light shone on that road: it dazzled him; it blinded him! He was felled to earth by the force of that atomic energy he had unwittingly invoked! He was not only blinded; he was temporarily paralyzed. Then he heard the voice: "Saul, Saul, why do you persecute me?" That was no figure of speech. It was no mere metaphorical language. We know the secret today. We have learned that when we persecute the friends of Jesus, we persecute Jesus! "Truly I tell you, just as you did ...to one of the least of these, you did ...it to me." (Matthew 25:40).

The Fact of Conversion

Then the amazing thing happens. You can't put your finger on a particular verse and say: "This is where Saul was converted!" It is a very rapid process, so rapid that events happen almost before you realize their significance, but you will find the scenario for this amazing drama well expressed in the ninth chapter of the Acts. Saul heard the voice: "I am Jesus, whom you are persecuting." (Acts 9:5) and later he heard that answer to his own prayer expressed in terms of command: "But get up and enter the city, and you will be told what you are to do." (Acts 9:6). It is the sign of sincerity in our conversion experience when we can pray, "Lord, what will you have me to do?" And the answer is always that we should do something about it. No treatment by a practitioner can take the place of obedience to that inner voice – that divine compulsion which rids us of our "compulsion neurosis." It doesn't have to come in such a violent or dramatic setting with all of us. It may come (it often has come) as we kneel before the altar at the climax of some church service. The dialogue between ourselves and the Master may be conducted in silence; but the essence of it will be the same as that between Saul and the Christ who challenged him. It will be realistic – the answer to our question, "Who are you, Lord?" But it will end with our own response to his command: "But get up and enter the city, and you will be told what you are to do." Follow this line fearlessly, courageously, and it will lead you to your divinely-decreed destiny.

Healing and Conversion Go Together

Saul's conversion was followed quickly by his healing – physically, mentally and spiritually. You might say that his conversion was actually a part of his healing, even including the healing of his eyes through the laying-on of the hands of Ananias.

We do not hear much about Ananias. Of course, we know be is no relation to the other Ananias, the husband of Sapphira, an entirely different person. He is a Christian disciple – not an apostle, just a disciple scared to death of Saul! So scared that even when the Lord comes in a vision and tells him to go to Saul, tells him what to say and what he is to do, he is almost afraid to carry it out and says, "Why, Lord, don't you know that this is the man who has been persecuting your followers? You want me to go and minister to *him*?" "Yes," says the Lord, "For he is an instrument whom I have chosen to bring my name before kings." (cf Acts 9:13-15). So Ananias becomes the humble, and rather reluctant channel through which this blessing is given. Finally, he gets the "green light" on it within himself and goes to Saul, gives him the message, and lifts him up, still blinded. Then comes great spiritual enlightenment and with it, his sight. "Brother Saul," says Ananias, laying his hands upon him, "Brother Saul... regain your sight." (Acts 9:17). Then, he introduces him to the household of faith, to the infant church.

What does all this mean for us today?

What does it mean for you who are seeking the healing of some long-standing trouble in your own life? Perhaps you have a local disorder, a painful malady, an emotional problem, or a family situation that gives you great distress. Or maybe you are at the end of your rope, facing economic disaster. You want to know whether Jesus Christ can heal such a malady as afflicts you now. Learn to put first things first. Seek Jesus for himself. Cry aloud (if it is really your deep desire) "Who are you, Lord?" Any specific prayer for relief or healing will simplify if you will seek Jesus first and bring your need into that realized presence. He will bring you wholeness, and in that wholeness you will find your specific and local solutions. When Jesus met Zaccheus, and that tax-gatherer responded to his challenge (not so very unlike the response of Saul) and invited Jesus to come home with him, Jesus exclaimed, "This day is salvation come to this house!" In Tyndale's translation (A.D. 1534) this verse reads: "This day is health come unto this house." (Luke 19:9). In original scriptures "salvation" always means "wholeness"; it is never a palliative; it is never a salve to give momentary relief, but a gift of new life to transform the entire nature of the patient. We find the same words in the Wycliffe Bible (much earlier than Tyndale). In Luke 1:77 for the words in the NRSV version, "To give knowledge of salvation to his people by the forgiveness of their sins," we have "To give the science of health unto his people by the remission of their sins." The science of health is the authentic knowledge of salvation in the most literal and remedial sense.

The "knowledge of salvation" is what you have always known it to be; but it is infinitely more than this! It includes all that the precious blood of Christ has accomplished and is accomplishing and will accomplish for us and in us! We use the words in this sense when we give the sacramental bread and wine to each communicant with the exhortation: "The blood of our Lord Jesus Christ... keep you in everlasting life!" If only we meant what we said; if only we would believe in the efficacy of this God-given medicine of the soul which can cure the body also! In seeking Christian healing we must of course get right with God before we begin praying for the physical healing. "But strive first for the kingdom of God, and his righteousness...!" (Matthew 6:33). But we don't stop there. We go right on to the "new person in Christ" which is his gift and which includes every description of healing ministry.

This is the greatest miracle of healing possible in our experience. "Let go... and let come!" Let go of the old self-seeking; yes, even let go of the seeking of "salvation" according to some obsolete formula. And "let come" the new pervasive life which flows through our veins as we receive this available medicine of God's love.

> **Let us pray:** Dear Father, we thank you for the way, the truth and the life revealed to us in Jesus Christ. We offer ourselves unreservedly to you. We pray that the love of Christ which passes knowledge may cleanse us from all the disease of sin. Work in us (as we are ready now) that great redemption, that great miracle of conversion, whereby we shall be no longer divided; whereby we shall be no longer wrong, inferior and unhappy, but by the grace of Jesus, and through his finished work, we shall become unified and right, superior and happy; for the kingdom and the power and the glory are yours forever and ever. Amen.

Questions

1. What is conversion? (p. 25-26; Acts 9:22,26)
2. What is the relationship between conversion and healing? (p. 30-31)
3. What is the difference between being healed and being cured?
4. What makes for a healing worship service on a Sunday morning? What is the most healing for you in the service?

III

HEALING AND FORGIVENESS

Then some people came, bringing to him [Jesus], a paralyzed man, carried by four of them. And when they could not bring him to Jesus because of the crowd, they removed the roof above him; and after having dug through it, they let down the mat on which the paralytic lay. When Jesus saw their faith, he said to the paralytic, "Son, your sins are forgiven." Now some of the scribes were sitting there, questioning in their hearts, "Why does this fellow speak this way? It is blasphemy! Who can forgive sins but God alone?" At once Jesus perceived in his spirit that they were discussing these questions among themselves, and he said to them, "Why do you raise such questions in your hearts? Which is easier, to say to the paralytic, 'Your sins are forgiven,' or to say, 'Stand up and take your mat and walk'? But so

> that you may know that the Son of Man has authority on earth to forgive sins" – he said to the paralytic – "I say to you, stand up, take your mat and go to your home." And he stood up, and immediately took the mat and went out before all of them; so that they were all amazed and glorified God saying "We have never seen anything like this!"
>
> – Mark 2:3-12

THIS STORY is told also in the ninth chapter of the Gospel of Matthew. Four friends bring a paralyzed man to Jesus. Their action is a beautiful and dramatic symbol of concern for others. The man is a pretty serious casualty – so paralyzed that he cannot even walk to Jesus. His condition is the result of his own shortcomings as is quite evident from the Bible story. The four men had courage, love and vicarious faith for their friend. We are not told that the paralytic had any faith. He may have had, but it is not stated. Jesus does not recognize faith in him, but he does see faith in the four friends who brought him.

This is a magnificent object lesson for a prayer group. Many times you must bring a person to Jesus in prayer who, as far as you can tell, does not have any faith, or if he has, it is very little. All right. Bring him.

Don't beg and beseech God to give him faith. Just bring him. That is all these four men did. They didn't preach to this man or tell him he would have to do this or that. They did not set any task before him. They just brought him. They somehow knew that if they could just get him into the immediate presence of Jesus, everything would be all right.

Some of us do not get our prayers answered because we are too much worried about it. We think we have to do a great deal. We sometimes do too much just as others do too little. It is a good thing to bring a person to Jesus and leave him there. Then, just watch and see what he will do for him!

What does Jesus do in this case? First of all, he does an outstanding piece of intuitional diagnosis. If you live near to God and have love in your heart, you will do quite a bit of this yourself. A mother usually doesn't have to read chapters of a doctor's book to find out what is wrong with her child. Nine times out of ten she knows. The tenth time she will look in the book only to corroborate what she knows anyway. Intuitional diagnosis is a method of love. It is, therefore, the method of God. Since Jesus was filled with the love of God, he did not have to use medical books. He knew without asking questions. In this case, he knew that the man's condition was due to sin. What that sin was, we do not know. We have the diagnosis in this story and the therapy follows. Jesus knowing the cause instantly knew the cure. The cure was implicit in the disease for one who knew so well how to read people. Most diseases are deficiency diseases. They are due to the lack of something. It may even be just a lack of love – or of faith. You have to give the positive that cancels out the negative. If you are a good spiritual therapist, you will know how much to give. If the disease is minus five, then you must give plus five of faith and love and prayer. If the disease is minus fourteen, then you must supply plus fourteen. Jesus did that. He saw this man needed just the absolute assurance of forgiveness. We are not even told that the man made any confession.

Then Jesus spoke four words to this man: the word of comfort, the word of release, the word of reason and the word of power. Let us consider them more closely.

The Word of Comfort

We use the word "comfort" to mean an expression of sympathy. It does not mean that at all. It means literally to strengthen. "Be of good courage" is one way of translating what Jesus first said to him. People sometimes become mentally ill for lack of encouragement. They may develop a guilt complex for the same reason. They think they are no good because nobody has ever told them that they are good. We should welcome every opportunity of giving encouragement. Not flattery. That is not encouragement. "Encourage" has as its root the French word for heart – "*coeur.*" So to encourage really means to enhearten. The Revised Standard Version of the Gospel of Matthew tells us Jesus said, "Take heart, my son." This is Jesus' first word to the man. "You don't have to worry. Your sins are forgiven." Coming from the lips of Jesus, the words had the authority of God himself, and the man knew it instinctively, though he may not have known who Jesus was.

If you cannot heal people, you might be a comfort to them and bring good cheer to them in the highest sense. If you have the love of Christ in your own life, learn to shed it abroad and make it available to others. You can give this strengthening word, "Be of good cheer." You can reinforce the courage of a person in need.

The Word of Release

But why be of good cheer? Because your sins are forgiven! "Oh," you say, "but I don't know that they are!" Well, don't you want them forgiven? Didn't Jesus come that he might take away the sins of the world? "Here is the Lamb of God, who takes away the sin of the world." (John 1: 29). That is what John the Baptist said. I believe that Jesus did something, something cosmic, something ultimate, something on the plane of reality whereby our sins may be forgiven. In other words, Jesus has set a credit balance for us on which we can draw by a simple act of faith.

There comes a time with sick people, especially those who are mentally or emotionally ill, when somebody needs to come in and speak an authoritative word of forgiveness so that it gets down into their subconscious mind and makes them know that the bondage which has held them and perhaps even caused their illness is broken. There are different ways of speaking this word. The old Methodist Class Meeting has one way. The Roman Catholic Church has its method. The Episcopal Church has its method. Modern evangelistic movements have their own methods which are sometimes rather unusual. But the object is the same – to release people from sin. If you can release people from sin, it is easy to release them from sickness and disease. Learn to speak the word of release.

I do not think these words, "Your sins are forgiven," ought to be limited to the clergy. Anyone who has the spirit of Jesus and is wholeheartedly and unselfishly concerned with releasing another person can give these words of release. These words must be said at the right time, under the right conditions, when the patient is ready and his mind is receptive. Sometimes an intolerable burden can be lifted from the heart of a person who is mentally or emotionally ill if they can just have the word of release – a great Word of Jesus.

But who are we to give such a word? Jesus gave this definite commission to his followers just before he went to heaven. Some may think that he limited it to the Apostles, but this cannot be insisted upon with certainty. One may as readily believe that he gave it to all his true followers. He said, "As my Father has sent me, so I send you." When he said this, he breathed on them, and said to them, "Receive the Holy Ghost. If you forgive the sins of any, they are forgiven them." (John 20:21-23). That is, if you forgive the sins of any, they are FORGIVEN. James echoed this in the fifth chapter of his epistle: "Are any among you sick? They should call for the elders of the church, and have them pray over them, anointing them with oil in the name of the Lord. The prayer of faith will save the sick and the Lord will raise them up; and anyone who has committed sins will be forgiven. Therefore confess your sins one to another and pray one for another, that you may be healed." (James 5:14-16). In 1 John 1:9 we read, "If we confess our sins, he who is faithful and just will forgive us our sins, and cleanse us from all unrighteousness." The Church is commissioned to give the word of release. We are all kings and priests unto God. We have a certain authority to speak in God's name. We must be ready to say as ministers or as God-appointed laypersons, "Your sins are forgiven."

This world is dying today for a lack of absolution, for the assurance of forgiveness. The one thing people want is a cure for sin and particularly a cure for the guilt complex. Many people are paying many dollars an hour to a psychiatrist to take away their guilt complex. Jesus gave his followers authority not only to cure disease but to absolve people from their sins. Jesus did absolve people and commissioned his disciples to continue this work. Absolution and healing go together. He breathes his spirit upon them as a prerequisite for the ministry of absolution. That has far reaching power. The Church has rightly inferred that whatever was given to the disciples was given to the Church for all time. I believe that is true.

I have spoken this word of release in all sorts of places – in hospitals, in jails, in mental hospitals, in normal circumstances and in unusual circumstances. It is a part of the pastoral ministry certainly. It ought to belong to the local pastor. It gives him a wonderful opportunity to bring release and even to start the process of healing in the minds and souls of people. I had one rather unique experience in Canada where a woman was healed of cancer through receiving absolution. In her case, which was peculiar, she was convinced that her cancer was a result of certain sins in her own life. It was a deep conviction. She felt that God had told her in church one Sunday night that she would have to get rid of that sin if she wanted to be healed. She did and she was healed. Do not read too much into this. Cancer is not always due to sin and certainly not to a sin of the flesh. Disease is not always due to the sin of the person who is ill. It is due to sin somewhere, but it may be way back in one's heredity, or it may be due to environment. It may have any number of causes. But sometimes it is the result of the sin of the patient, and if that should happen to be true, if the patient gets rid of the sin, he or she may get rid of the disease.

Some years ago I had an opportunity to study Sanskrit. I didn't get very far. It is a language you pick up very slowly. One night we were studying a certain word and the teacher said, "Of course, the word that really should be used in translating this is 'absolve.' That is what it means. Absolve is the verb and absolution is the noun. There is Dr. Banks over there. He will understand this. What would you say 'absolve' means in English, Dr. Banks?" I told her, Then she gave me some new light! She said, "Well, that's what it means in Sanskrit." Then her face lighted up and she added, "Of course, there is a still further meaning! That word in Sanskrit really means 'to lift above limitation.'" When Jesus said, "Your sins are forgiven," I suddenly saw that he was not saying, "Just forget about it!" He was literally lifting the patient above those limitations that were holding him in bondage. Absolution is related to the word "absolute." In our philosophy, God is the absolute. Why is he the absolute? Because he is above all limitations! So to absolve people is to lift them above the limitation of sin and all that sin entails, through the mighty power of God!

The Word of Reason

Now, the word of release would have been sufficient. That would have ended the story so far as the healing was concerned. But there was interruption and interference and it came as usual from the enemies of Jesus. They brought in a theological red herring! And this red herring was drawn across the scene to attract the attention of the crowd because our Lord's enemies did not want the crowd to accept his teaching. I am sorry to say that theology is still brought into this field sometimes as a red herring to distract people from simple healing as Jesus taught it. There is an authentic theology of healing for those who want to take it up. But too often theology is brought in not to help healing but to question it. It covers up the lamentable lack of spiritual therapy in the lives and ministry of the modern church. That is a sharp statement but I do not make it unkindly. This is rapidly being corrected. A few years ago a close friend of mine wrote his seminary thesis on the subject of Christian healing and it was read before the whole school. Younger people in the ministry are seeing increasingly that Jesus' healing method was not unscientific. It is not contrary to the laws of medicine, or to the laws of the mind, or to the accumulated wealth of psychological knowledge. It can be blended with all these things. Immanuel Episcopal Church in Boston has a counseling service, but it also has services of healing where people come to the altar and prayer is offered for them. This might be said of many other churches perhaps, but I happen to know about Immanuel Church. Jesus' way of healing is not confined to a few radical cults today. It is getting into the mind and conscience of the church and finding expression in the worship and activity of the church.

Jesus does not despise the word of reason. He would not give it first place perhaps. Some people want a religion of emotion, but there is an important minority who do want to use their reason, who do not want their religion entirely predigested. You are doing yourself an injustice if you feed your soul entirely on predigested food. It would be good for you to do a little mental work. Get your mental faculties involved in your relationship with God.

So the scribes were not at fault in using their reason. The fault lay in the way they used it. They said, "Why does this fellow speak in this way? It is blasphemy! Who can forgive sins but God alone?" (Mark 2:7). I can see the pious look on their faces, can't you? Weren't they good boys? Didn't they know the law of Moses perfectly? Wasn't Jesus a heretic talking about forgiving people their sins?

But their purpose did not work out! Jesus took them up on their question and answered them directly, not by appealing to their emotions but by appealing to their reason. There is a subtle touch here. There is a fine piece of diagnosis, not of the sick man now, but of the priests when Jesus says, "Why do you think evil in your hearts?" Matthew prefaces these words with the observation, "Jesus, knowing their thoughts, said, 'Why do you raise such questions in your hearts?'" But you don't think with your heart! You feel with your heart. You think with your head! What did Jesus mean when he said, "Why do you raise such questions in your hearts?" It is a clever question. It pictures what many of us do today. We allow the heart to control the head. We allow the feelings to dictate our thoughts instead of allowing our thoughts to dictate our feeling. They had allowed their feelings to run away with them. People let their feelings run away with them because they do not have a right judgment.

These men ought to have known better. They had been trained and were members of the Sanhedrin – some of them at least. They knew the law of Moses and all the scriptures. Yet they allowed their feelings of resentment, jealousy and hatred against Jesus to control their thoughts. And so they said, "Why does this fellow speak this way? It is blasphemy!" But they did not pull the wool over Jesus' eyes. He knew what they were thinking! He gave a great formula for spiritual therapy which we ought never to forget. He said, "Which is easier, to say to the paralytic, 'Your sins are forgiven,' or to say, 'Stand up and take your mat and walk'? But that you may know that the Son of Man has authority on earth to forgive sins–he then said to the paralytic 'I say to you, stand up, take your mat and go to your home.'" THAT YOU ALL MAY KNOW! Not that you may feel but that you all may know. The disciple's way is to know. It was a master stroke. It absolutely silenced the critics. There wasn't a thing they could say. It took all the wind out of their sails. It robbed them of all their arrows of venom and spite.

The word of reason is that you may know! If there is a time when you are depressed, if some fear has overcome you for the moment, if some sin has you temporarily in its grip, if some means of grace to which you have clung has failed, remember this formula, "that you may know that the Son of Man has power on earth to forgive sins." He is the Son of God and the Son of Man. He is the one who has perfectly identified himself with the whole race. He has carried the whole weight of responsibility for all our sins. He has borne our sins on the Tree in his own body. The chastisement of our peace was upon him and by his stripes we are healed. And now, the Son of Man has power on earth NOW to forgive sins. Learn that! It is the word that will give you absolute release. It is the word of reason as well as the word of release.

The Word of Power

Which is easier – to get rid of the symptom or to cure the cause of disease? Well, you must have both. If you can get rid of the cause, the symptom will take care of itself. Jesus says then to the paralytic, "Get up and prove to yourself and show these people that your sins really are forgiven." Some people find forgiveness of sin and healing simultaneously. When they receive the forgiveness of sin, then physical, mental and moral release come together. More often, however, the moral and mental and physical release comes after the word of forgiveness. Actually we have the latent power to do (after we have been forgiven) the thing we could not do before. We must learn to speak this word of power to ourselves and to others. Sometimes people who have been unacquainted with the words of Jesus receive more from them in the way of healing power than we receive who have known his words all our lives. We have heard his words so often. We assume we know what they mean. We assume that we believe them. Often we do not. They come to those who have not heard them with a freshness and reality that may evoke a response which we fail to give.

Learn to release yourself and your neighbor by saying about him only what God says. Learn to bring release by the help of God. Speak TRUTH about your neighbor. There is danger of going off on a metaphysical tangent, and yet the metaphysical teachers have a good lesson for us on this. When you say unkind things about your neighbor, you are not really telling the truth. Those unkind things you say are not the TRUTH. You mean – they are facts! But facts are not necessarily TRUTH. Nothing that can be destroyed is true in the ultimate sense. Only that which is permanent is really true. The faults, the failings, the little bad habits, the little superficial weaknesses of people that we sometimes dwell upon and discuss – these are not the TRUTH about them.

So speak TRUTH about the person whose healing you desire – yourself or another. Tell people that they can be free. Tell them that there is a part of them that is free right now, that even if they have been physically ill for five years, yet there is an essential truth about them that is absolutely health-giving, that is in accord with the original blueprints of God in their creation. "The right hand of the Lord has triumphed! The right hand of the Lord is exalted! The right hand of the Lord has triumphed!" (Psalms 118:16 – ***The Book of Common Prayer***, 1928). I love to say that when I am praying for healing. There are many marvelous statements of TRUTH in the Bible. Dig them out! Make a list of them! There is a tremendous force for righteousness and health and peace of mind in these affirmations. The Psalms are full of them. Others are given in other parts of this book.

There are people who seriously need healing. They are asking for it. They are praying for it. They need a little help. We have these four words. Let us give them the reinforcement of our own faith and love. Let us give them the word of comfort, the word of release, the word of reason, the word of power.

> **Let us pray:** Dear Father in Heaven, speak your Word to each one of us today. Speak to me and to all others who are reading this book the word of comfort – "Be of good cheer!" May we know that we have a way out of sin and depression in your holy word. Speak to us the word of release– "Your sins are forgiven." And help us to receive this not alone for ourselves, but to be ready

upon your signal to say to somebody else– "Your sins are forgiven." Speak to us the word of reason. Speak to us the word of power that we may know – not guess, but know that the Son of Man has power on earth, power here, now, TODAY, as I read this prayer – power to forgive sin. Bid us "Rise, take up [our] bed, and walk." Bid us do the thing we thought we couldn't do. Bid us do the things that used to be impossible–until we heard your word. We now use this power and we thank you for it and we will glorify you in ministering to other lives. Amen.

QUESTIONS

1. In the Scripture on pages 35-36, what is the relationship between healing and forgiveness of sins? In John 5:14, Jesus also mentions a link between healing and sin? Also look up what is said about this in John 9:1, the man born blind, and Luke 13:10, the woman bent double.
2. Can you think of two or three people who need to know that their sins are forgiven? How could you let them know it based on pages 38-41?

3. Think of a person who is difficult for you to be around. What is the truth about him or her?

IV

A TECHNIQUE OF DEDICATION

> I appeal to you therefore, brothers and sisters, by the mercies of God, to present your bodies as a living sacrifice, holy and acceptable to God, which is your spiritual worship. – Romans 12:1

THIS is what the Apostle Paul believed every Christian should do with his body: he should present it to God as a living sacrifice. In the service of Holy Communion the priest or minister says on behalf of all of us: "Here we offer and present unto you, O Lord, our selves, our souls and bodies, to be a reasonable, holy, and living sacrifice to you." You have heard these words perhaps dozens of times. You have given personal assent to them. But have you ever seriously meditated over their meaning? This is no mechanical act to which we are called nor is it just a little touch of ritual. The summons is to an intelligent offering of ourselves.

I have found out by experience that this self-giving is accomplished more successfully if it is done slowly and thoughtfully. You dedicate your head which represents your thinking. You offer your eyes which represent your seeing, your ears which represent your hearing, your mouth, lips, tongue which represent your speaking, your heart which represents your emotional drives. One might go on and on, picturing this process of presenting the body to God. We know today that there is a close relationship and interdependence between the body and soul. When you intelligently dedicate the body, you are dedicating the soul's work because the body and soul are so inextricably related to each other that you cannot offer one without offering the other. The body expresses, or crystallizes, or externalizes, the creative work of the soul. In a way the body is the sacrament of the soul. It is the projection of the soul. The great Elizabethan poet, Edmund Spenser, in his "Ode to Beauty," puts this thought into two lines:

> For of the soul the body form doth take
> For soul is form and doth the body make.

Other poets and philosophers have expressed the same concept. The dedication of the physical body has far-reaching implications as we shall now see by considering the dedication of various parts of it.

The Dedication of the Breathing

We are told in the first book of the Bible that the Lord God breathed into man's nostrils the breath of life, and man became a living soul. (Genesis 2:7). Every Bible student ought to have a good concordance. Many of the more expensive Bibles have a small concordance in the back, but Young's ***Analytical Concordance*** is the standard work of its kind. It is rather expensive, but in it you can locate easily every single thing the Bible has to say about any subject which interests you. It is complete. With this book, even though you are working by yourself, you can get together a vast store of information as to what the Bible teaches about the various parts of the body. You will be amazed at the discoveries to be made in this field. In the book of Job we find, "But truly it is the spirit in a mortal, the breath (inbreathing) of the Almighty, that makes for understanding." (Job 32:8).

What we need is a good deep-breathing exercise for the soul which will enable us to breathe in (literally) the very life of God. The hymn, "Breathe on me, Breath of God," is such a deep-breathing exercise for the soul.

> Breathe on me. Breath of God: fill me with
> life anew, That I may love what Thou dost
> love, and do what Thou wouldst do.
> Breathe on me. Breath of God, until my

> heart is pure, Until with Thee I will one will, to do or to endure.
> Breathe on me. Breath of God, till I am wholly Thine, Till all this earthly part of me glows with Thy fire divine.
> Breathe on me, Breath of God, so shall I never die. But live with Thee the deathless life of Thine Eternity.

Breathe deeply as you think through the first line of each stanza of this hymn. As the natural air fills the lungs and purifies the blood, picture to yourself the Holy Spirit of God entering into your very soul, at the invitation of your fervent but not strained desire, cleansing your heart and mind and quickening all their activities. Exhale slowly as you think through the second line of each stanza, and let your outgoing breath symbolize to you the sharing with the world around you of that divine life which you have just received. A careful study of this hymn will show you that the first line of each stanza of the hymn represents the breathing-in of God's gracious inspiration and the second line represents the effect of this in and through your own life. The filling of the lungs should be accompanied by your reception of God's creative word and the emptying of the lungs with its expression. The great prayer which many of us use near the beginning of the service of Holy Communion shows the same sequence: "Almighty

God, to you all hearts are open, all desires known, and from you no secrets are hid: Cleanse the thoughts of our hearts by the inspiration of your Holy Spirit, that we may perfectly love you, and worthily magnify your holy name; through Christ our Lord. Amen."

Or take another illustration: The breathing apparatus of the body becomes a perpetually active radio station, receiving and sending out the living Word of God. Quietly listen to these words of God's Holy Spirit, receiving them into your heart: "BE STILL, AND KNOW THAT I AM GOD." (Psalms 46:10). "Give yourself wholly to me that my inspiration may fill your mind, your heart, your soul, your very senses. I quicken you to know me, think me, feel me, see me, hear me. Be still and know that I am God."

Then let your soul breathe out this answer: "Father, I offer my entire body to you as a living sacrifice, as an authentic temple of the Holy Spirit. Make it a member of Christ's body. Help me to glorify you in my body and in my spirit, for they are both yours." There is healing in such prayer and dedication.

The Dedication of the Heart

The most important thing to dedicate in your whole body is the heart. I don't, of course, mean just the organ that pumps the blood through the body. That is important, and by all means dedicate it.

Many people have mild forms of heart trouble in this age of tremendous stimulation. Don't worry over minor symptoms. Learn to relax. Pray something like this: "O God, thank you for this wonderful instrument that pumps the blood, the very fluid of life, all over my body. Thank you for its tireless work. Thank you for keeping it on the job day and night." I find that if we really love people in an unselfish, outgoing way, that will do more for disturbed heart-action than some medical treatments. When we really love people, they usually love us back. It works on a reciprocal basis. So don't worry about minor symptoms. The book of Proverbs has some good affirmations showing the relationship between a happy, loving outlook on life and health of body: "A cheerful heart is a good medicine: but a downcast spirit dries up the bones." (Proverbs 17:22). Moffatt translates this: "A glad heart helps and heals: a broken spirit saps vitality."[1] Or here is another: "A glad heart makes a cheerful countenance: but by sorrow of the heart the spirit is broken... a cheerful heart has a continual feast." (Proverbs 15:13, 15b).

There are twelve hundred verses in the Bible referring to the heart. "God is the strength in my heart," the Psalmist says, "and my portion forever." (Psalms

1 From The Bible–A New Translation by James Moffatt. Copyright 1922 - 1935 and 1950 by Harper & Brothem. Used by permission.

73:26). That is a marvelous verse to ponder, to affirm for yourself and to make a part of your own experience. Frequently in the Bible, the heart is regarded as the center of the emotions, feelings or affections. In the deepest sense the dedication of the heart is the dedication of the affections to God. This prayer will help you.

> My Father, I love you with all my heart and with all my soul and with all my strength. I thank you for the wonderful service and faithfulness of this organ of circulation which keeps the bloodstream pulsating throughout my body! Even more I thank you for the ability to love – for my part in the sacred heart of Jesus which yearns in love over all mankind. May my heartbeat be attuned to that great heart of compassion! Let me keep my heart with all diligence, for out of it are the issues of life. O God, you are the strength of my heart and my portion for ever. Amen.

Moffatt translates the familiar verse "Keep your heart with all vigilance, for from it flow the springs of life" in this arresting way: "Guard above all things, guard your inner self, for so you live and prosper." (Proverbs 4:23).

A word needs to be said to Protestants about that expression "the sacred heart of Jesus." "The sacred heart of Jesus" is a very beautiful and meaningful phrase, that Protestants are not familiar with. The sacred heart of Jesus is the outgoing compassion of Jesus for all mankind. It is the love of Jesus poured out for the redemption of the world-healing, saving, helping. This love of Christ for the whole world goes out and redeems, renovates, replenishes, restores, heals, brings back and rescues. So the little prayer to share in the sacred heart of Jesus is our petition to share in all these wonderful things that he does.

Jesus brought to earth a wholly new standard of love which he set up for all his followers in his parting commandment: "As the Father has loved me, so I have loved you... Love each other, as I have loved you." (John 15:9, 12). Until then, man had been commanded to love God with all his heart and mind and soul and strength, and his neighbor as himself. But now he is told that he is to love in a new way, with a new kind of heart, mind, soul and strength, none other than the heart, mind, soul and strength of Christ himself which he would actually bestow upon all who would receive him in exchange for themselves. Here is a gift of inconceivable magnitude. He promises to endow us with a God-like way of loving by imparting to us his own divine nature. (See 2

Peter 1:4). He gives us the Father's love to him, and bids us give that love to others. And lest we should not dare to believe such overwhelming words, he confirms them several times as in John 14:21-23; John 17:23-26. Human love is not enough for the sons of God. They are commanded to love divinely! What a calling! Not in some future state of bliss, but here and now on this sad, sorrow-laden earth! To love as God loves us in Christ, the only-begotten and the well-beloved! And we receive this love on no other terms than willingness to receive such love as the free gift of God. It is for this kind of love that we are asking when we dedicate our hearts as a living sacrifice, holy and acceptable unto God.

The Dedication of the Eyes and Ears

In the divine psychology of Jesus, the right use of eye and ear is essential to right judgment. Jesus tells us that his judgment is righteous because he seeks not his own will but the will of him that sent him, that he judges as he hears and sees the Father, not according to appearances. This is a fulfillment of Isaiah 11:2-4: "The spirit of the Lord shall rest on him… and he shall not judge by what his eyes see, or decide by what his ears hear; but with righteousness he shall judge." So Jesus has given us a picture of the way our eyes and ears ought to be used – by presenting them to God as a living sacrifice, by seeking to see and hear everything in the light of God's will. Here are two good prayers: "Open my eyes so that I may behold wondrous things out of your law!" (Psalms 119:18). And "Speak, Lord; for your servant is listening." (I Samuel 3:9). We are told that the Lord opens the eyes of the blind and that he opens the ears of the deaf. We need a divine kind of seeing and hearing if we are to do the work of our Father in this world.

Carry such questions as these through the day with you: "How is Christ looking at this? How will he use these eyes if I remember that they belong to him?" See people with the eyes of Christ when your natural self sees them only as "problems." You will then see the most "difficult" people as immeasurably dear to God since he gave himself in his only-begotten Son that they should not perish but have everlasting life. If we would look more profoundly, more deeply, into people, we would see the divine image there, obscured perhaps by sin, but still there. And that very recognition would enable us to help the person become normal spiritually. "Blessed are the eyes that see the things that you see," Jesus said. (Luke 10:23). And again, "If your eye is healthy, your whole body will be full of light." (Matthew 6:22).

The new birth from above opens a new faculty in the soul – the power to listen inwardly and spiritually. This kind of listening is sometimes called contemplation. The Bible describes this in various ways – "beholding the glory of the Lord," "listening carefully to his voice," and in other ways which you will come to recognize from your own personal study of the Bible. Here are some prayers that will help you to receive healing both for your physical and your spiritual eyes and ears: "Thank God for the gift of vision, for the inscrutable mystery of my eyes, for the great services rendered by these wonderful friends all through the years! Father, I thank you for vision and for the miracle of sight! Help me to see the potential perfection of everything and everyone within my range of vision!" And "Thank God for my ears and for the faculty of hearing! Speak, Lord, for your servant hears! Make me a better listener – swift to hear, slow to speak, slow to anger! Make me more sensitive to the voice of your Spirit in the silence!" It is that growing sensitiveness to the presence of the healing Christ that prepares us and fills us with the expectation of receiving his gifts. And the best preparation we can make is the dedication of our bodies to God.

The Dedication of the Hands and Feet

The hands express the will. They carry into action the decisions which we make. Desire and imagination act together to give us a mental picture of an object or course of action. If reason, faith or emotion approve this picture, the will consents to it, and the hand will be the agent which translates it finally into fact.

The hand is the sign of man's power to make. This power to make is man's likeness to the creative power of God, and bears eloquent witness to that divine nature from which he has "fallen by self will," and can only regain through being "born anew of water and of the Spirit."

The true purpose of your hands is to serve the will of God, as the hands of Jesus served to bring the kingdom of the Father on earth as in heaven. And since to every man is given according to his work, we can only be sure that our handiwork is approved of God if desire, imagination and will are dedicated to him – disciplined, directed and ruled by his Holy Spirit. Then, and then only, dare we pray with Moses, the man of God: "Let the favor of the Lord our God be upon us, and prosper for us the work of our hands– O prosper the work of our hands." (Psalms 90:17). The fact that Jesus cast out demons with the "finger of God" revealed the present reality of the kingdom of God. (Luke 11:20).

The true office of the feet is, as in the case of St. Christopher, to be Christ-bearers, carrying his presence into every place, and waiting always upon his direction. Ponder this injunction in Ephesians 6:15, having "as shoes for your feet, put on whatever will make you ready to proclaim the gospel of peace," and these words from the prophet Isaiah: "How beautiful upon the mountains are the feet of the messenger who announces peace, who brings good news; who announces salvation." (Isaiah 52:7). Another wonderful promise is that God will guide our feet into the way of peace. (Luke 1:79). Then pray this little prayer:

> Teach my hands your way of serving;
> Teach my feet your way of walking.

A Living Sacrifice

Look at the cross and see yourself (your old, troublesome self) crucified there with Christ. And see your true self, redeemed and restored in him, united to his body, the Church – refreshed, restored, re-invigorated with his very body and blood, and going forth to live his life and to do his work in the world. That is a high ideal, but not too high – for it is his will and "in his will is our peace." You can get no peace or happiness or permanent comfort in the real sense outside of God's will. "You have made us for yourself and our hearts are restless until they rest in you."

The spirit in Christ is the same spirit which today clothes the Church with dynamic power whenever it rises to the full measure of its privilege and responsibility. Surely there is in this food for reflection, and we shall not be unresponsive to our Lord's contemporary demand for cooperation. He needs our bodies for the transmission of his power, our lips to speak his words full of healing energy, our hands to do his works of compassion, our hearts as radioactive centers for his great love for persons, and the obligation of our whole beings that the incarnation may actually be extended and projected through his Church today. "And here we offer and present to you, O Lord, ourselves, our souls and bodies... to be a reasonable, holy and living sacrifice to you." If this intention were carried into every approach to the altar and to life there would soon be such a manifestation of power in the Church as has never yet been known.

How May I Experience This Power in My Own Life?

The answer is very simple. Stretch out your hand and touch Christ. This advice may be accepted symbolically by some, metaphysically by others, and intuitively by still more. The terminology does not matter. We will touch him in the sacrament of holy communion, and as we receive the sacred elements and hear the wondrous words: "Preserve your body and soul," will receive his perfect wholeness. Others will touch him by the act of conscious realization, possibly by the repeated affirming of Christ's in-dwelling presence in long hours of silence. Still others will find him and touch him through the members of his body on earth (whether clergy or laity).

> The healing of His seamless dress
> Is by our beds of pain;
> We touch Him in life's throng and press
> And we are whole again.
>
> – Whittier

Basil Wilberforce says,

> Jesus Christ was the manifestation in a visible form of the accessibility, helpfulness and nearness of God. God and man met in him. He laid the hands of God in healing power upon the whole of humanity, and sanctified its entire life. The arms that opened to the little children, the hands that touched the lepers, the feet that were washed in the harlot's tears were God's. Jesus was the sacrament of God; the certified channel through which the love of God was poured forth, the outward and visible sign of an inward and spiritual omnipotence. The organization which he founded and which was called the Church, was to be in like manner the sacrament of himself.

See yourself in Christ; know yourself to be a partaker of his perfect atonement, of the rich provision he has made for your complete redemption, and as you enter into this realization you will be like the woman Jesus healed of a serious hemorrhage who "felt in her body that she was healed."

> **Let us pray.** God the Father bless you. God the Son heal you. God the Holy Spirit sanctify you. May your whole spirit and soul and body be preserved blameless unto the coming of Jesus Christ. So it shall be and so it is. Amen.

Questions

1. Read the song and prayers through on pages 53-56. Pray them through several times.
2. Which scripture means the most to you in the section about Dedication of the heart? (p. 55-58)
3. Try to see and hear through the eyes of God for one day (p. 61-63).
4. Do one thing this week that you feel specifically "called" to do.

V

WILL THERAPY

Faith and Will Power

> As he approached Jericho, a blind man was sitting by the roadside begging. When he heard a crowd going by, he asked what was happening. They told him, "Jesus of Nazareth is passing by." Then he shouted, "Jesus, Son of David, have mercy on me!" Jesus stood still and ordered the man to be brought to him; and when he came near, he asked him, "What do you want me to do for you?" He said, "Lord, let me see again." Jesus said to him, "Receive your sight; your faith has saved you." Immediately he regained his sight and followed him, glorifying God; and all the people, when they saw it, praised God.
>
> – Luke 18:35–43

THIS STORY illustrates the tremendous power of *will therapy*. I was introduced to this some years ago in a book shop when I picked up a book entitled, ***Will Therapy***. It was written by a great psychiatrist, Otto Rank, of Berlin, Germany, a former associate of Freud of Vienna. There is a story back of that book that throws light on the subject of this chapter.

Otto Rank, at the time he was associated with Freud, stopped in to see him at his office one day. He met a lady coming out and recognized her. He had seen her there before. She was one of Freud's regular patients. When he got inside, he said, "Herr Freud, hasn't that lady been coming to you for quite some time?"

"Oh, yes," said Freud, "She's been coming here a long time!"

"Well, how long has she been coming for treatments? "

"Oh, about three years!"

"THREE YEARS!" Rank exclaimed. "Is she cured?"

"No!" Freud answered. "She's not cured."

"Will she ever be cured?" questioned Dr. Rank.

"No – probably not!" Freud answered.

"Well, but you still take her money! You still encourage her to come for treatments?"

"Oh yes," said Freud, "I'm very much interested. I shall probably write a book about her."

This made Dr. Rank do some very thorough heart-searching. He went away with a feeling of righteous indignation. "What's wrong here?" he asked himself. Freud had done some marvelous analyses of that woman. Yet, Rank pondered, he has never aroused her *will* into cooperation. And he was right – that was the trouble. Freud had done a beautiful diagnosis. He was going to write a book about this woman, but he had not cured her. This, of course, is not to criticize psychologists; we have much to learn from them.

Dr. Rank separated himself from Freud, set up his own office and began to work with this idea of will therapy, later publishing the book which I found. When his patients came to him, he would take out his notebook and pen, make a preliminary examination and diagnosis, look up at the patient and say, "With full cooperation you should be well in – say three months! Will you work with me toward a perfect cure in three months?" The patient would usually answer, "Yes, doctor." He would put that down and mark the date in his book. He tells us in one of his writings that most of his patients got well even before the date they agreed upon with him. That was will therapy. He aroused and enlisted the will of the patient right from the beginning. Dr. Rank's method also involved a powerful auto-suggestion, looking towards recovery. The patient's cure began when he could say, "I *will* to be well; I will work to this end and expect to succeed in this purpose."

The Bible story at the beginning of this chapter is a delightful bit of case history. There are many in the four gospels. Jesus was not a magician nor a fraud. He was a master at diagnosis and cure. In this case, he uses will therapy.

But let us look at the story. Here is a blind man. When a person loses the power of one sense faculty, the other senses are augmented. They are on the job more than ever. So although this blind man cannot see Jesus, he nevertheless has a pretty shrewd idea of what is going on. He knows, by a sort of sixth sense, that this is his one superlative opportunity of getting healed. If he lets this opportunity slip by, it will never come back to him. He is absolutely right. So what does he do? Hearing the multitudes, he cries out, catching their enthusiasm. He realizes that he is even now almost in the presence of this great healer. What he hears stimulates his faith. "Faith comes by hearing," and if you really listen to the truth of God as it is given by faithful witnesses, that hearing will arouse your faith. When you have faith, you have the currency that pays for healing.

I learned this lesson – that faith is the currency that pays for healing – from a British engineer in Egypt. He was knighted by the King of England. He had a job of irrigating the Nile Delta. His name was Sir William Willcocks. I carried on a long correspondence with him over a period of six or seven years and still have some of his letters. He had a most amazing gift of healing. He could heal those natives, although he was a British engineer – not a missionary nor a clergyman – for he had marvelous faith. He said to me, "Faith is the recognized currency of the spiritual world. If you have enough faith, it is like having a pocketful of money. You can buy things with it."

Faith is the recognized currency of the spiritual world! "Well," you say to yourself, "give us more faith!" Paul said, "Faith comes by hearing." Listen! Really listen with ears and heart and will and understanding to the truth of God and you will get that faith. How does this blind man get it? He discovers a very simple truth. It is one of those obvious things so close to you that you don't see it. It is like the saying that you can't see the woods for the trees. He discovers that wherever Jesus Christ is, there is healing power. That has been true for nineteen centuries. That is why in a healing mission we sing many songs and choruses about Jesus. That is why we often speak of him. We know from long experience that wherever

Jesus is, there is healing power. The very story of Jesus, the name of Jesus, the very echo of his words, the concentration of attention and desire on him open the door for healing. That is a very simple, very obvious fact, but we don't use it as we might. This little chorus helps to focus our attention on him:

> O it is Jesus! O it is Jesus! Yes, it is Jesus in my soul, For I have touched the hem of his garment, And his love has made me whole.
>
> – An old Negro spiritual

Some "intellectuals" will say, "That's just sentimental stuff! People sing those choruses because of the emotional satisfaction it gives them." Maybe! But that is not the whole explanation! The songs about Jesus cause people to think about Jesus and when they think about Jesus, they are likely to meet him. And if they meet him and get close enough to him, they cannot help being healed. Everybody who comes close to Jesus and *wills* to be united with him will be healed. It follows as the night the day.

But let us go on with the story. "Jesus of Nazareth is passing by." That is a marvelous text for a sermon, but what do you get out of it? Is it just a bit of Bible history, or a Bible quotation, or is there more to it than that? As you read it, it is in the present tense. Let's think about it that way – not that he did pass by or will pass by, but that he is passing by. Jesus passes by in the regular cycle of the church year, of the Christian year. Every Christmas is a call to be reborn in Jesus. Every Epiphany which follows Christmas is a period for the manifesting of Jesus. Every Lent is a firm challenge to set aside those things which keep us away from him. Every Easter, Jesus of Nazareth passes by – risen from the dead, triumphant over the grave. It is important that we develop that fourth dimensional way of reading the gospels. I do not mean anything philosophical by that. I just mean that we eradicate the time and space elements in our reading. And we are no longer seeing Jesus of long ago who walked in the village streets. We are seeing the living Lord who walks the streets of our own city. Jesus is before your eyes and you are a part of that scene. With a little practice, you can read the gospels in this way. You can react just as realistically as any character in the story. The great conversions that you hear about and the great healings that you hear about usually come because the person so healed or so evangelized is lifted above the limitations of time and space. That can happen to you. Jesus of Nazareth is passing by.

What did the blind man say? He said the only thing he could say. He called out, "JESUS! Son of David, have mercy on me." I cannot give you an exposition of those words. You don't get their meaning by any theological studies. You wouldn't learn it from clever explanations. It is a cry of the soul. It is a person reaching up for the hand of God, stretched out to help him. "Jesus, Son of David, have mercy on me."

The crowd rebukes him. That is one of the most amazing things to me. It is one of the things I don't understand and never have understood: there is frequently more hindrance to the ministry of healing within organized churches than there is on the outside. There are people in every church who are ultraconservative and they say, "Healing? That is the doctor's job. It is not our job in the church. Leave it alone. You are trespassing. We don't want you bringing Christian Science into the church. If you want to heal, go outside and do it. If you are sick, go out and talk to a doctor." That attitude is changing and there is a new emphasis on healing as a part of the total task of the Christian Church, a commission given to her by our Lord himself. We must work by prayer and by consecrated common sense to show orthodox Christian people that the healing power of Jesus is an essential part of the Christian Gospel and not something imported from the outside. It will not disintegrate a church; it will build up a church. In this story, the very disciples and followers of Jesus, with mistaken zeal, discourage this man from coming and asking for his healing. They did not think this beggar should interfere with the proper routine work of Jesus. The crowd thought he was making a noise that was interfering with the peace. He was obstructing the procession. And they tried to hush him up, but the more they rebuked him, the louder he cried, "Jesus, Son of David, have mercy on me." He kept it up.

Then, Jesus comes to the forefront of the picture. He doesn't say anything to the disciples. He probably forgave them. It was just mistaken zeal, mistaken loyalty to him, an attempt to keep him from extra worry and trouble. Jesus stopped and he commanded this man to be brought to him and they brought him. Jesus stopped the whole crowd in order to talk to one man. It is a thrilling episode.

Then Jesus tests this man. Our Lord's question was not asked out of idle curiosity. Jesus knew what the man wanted! Yes! But he had to evoke the response from this man's will. Jesus was a master of *will therapy*. He asks, not a polite question essentially, but a searching question – "What do you want? What do you will?" In other words, "Is your will for recovery in line with the will of God that I represent?" We all have some faith for healing, but have we acquired the will to focus that faith? Right back comes the answer of the blind, "Lord, let me see again." I venture to think that although this man was probably a peasant and uneducated, his whole mind vas completely concentrated on this thought – no other thought entered into it.

I wonder sometimes about our prayers – our private prayers as well as our public prayers. I wonder how much we have learned the art of concentration. You do not really meditate unless you concentrate. The art of meditation is to keep the mind on one thing for a given period. It is an art; it has to be acquired. Let me illustrate this by a story.

About a hundred years ago there was a Spanish monk going around on a donkey through southern Spain. As he was approaching one little cross-roads village, a peasant on foot met him. He said, "Good morning, Father."

The monk responded, "Good morning, my son."

And the peasant said, "What are you doing, Father?"

To which the monk replied, "I'm meditating, my son."

"Oh, you're meditating! Well, that's easy! Anybody can meditate."

"No, my son, it's very hard to meditate, especially on a hot day and riding on a donkey over these bad roads."

"And you're meditating, Father?"

"Yes, I'm meditating," said the monk.

"Oh, well, I still think it's easy. Anybody – even I – can meditate."

The monk looked at him rather charitably and then said, "My son, if you will get down on your knees and meditate for three minutes on the love of God, I'll give you this donkey."

The face of the peasant brightened up and he could imagine himself already in possession of the donkey. So, he got down on his knees, clasped his hands and closed his eyes. His lips began to move silently as though in rapt meditation. But three minutes? That's a long time! At the end of one minute's meditation, he suddenly opened his eyes and said, "Do I get the saddle as well, Father?"

We smile at the peasant, but how often have we said, "Now, I'm going to have five minutes uninterrupted communion with God." And we start with good intentions. Then, we begin to think – what am I going to have for breakfast? Did I finish answering that letter I started the other day? And a dozen incidental, trivial things keep coming in, invading the mind and challenging our ability to keep the mind on the things of God. It is not easy to meditate. "No, my son," – like the monk, I say – "it is not easy to meditate."

Meditation is not a striving or a struggling to coerce yourself into action, however. It is rather a deliberate setting of the eyes towards a definite goal. It is a voluntary concentration of the eyes of the soul upon higher objectives. The mystic would say it was the concentration of the eyes of the soul upon God. You look toward the source of power and immediately your will is recharged. True meditation becomes contemplation, and as Ruysbroeck reminds us, "We contemplate what we are and we are what we contemplate, since, our essence, losing nothing of its distinctive individuality is united to that divine truth that respects diversity." Some will achieve this focusing of the will by turning to the divine presence within; others will attain a similar result by contemplating some great work of nature or by meditating before a beautiful altar in a quiet sanctuary. Persius, a Roman poet of the first century, affirmed: "What you strive for is within you, seek it not without."

There is great reward in meditation. When we really learn to set our minds on God and seek God for himself and love him supremely and realize how marvelous he is and recall the meaning of prayer – the enthusiasm for God's presence, the thrill of God's self-revelation to us – we ought to be moved to heartfelt prayer. "Lord, let me see again." It is the climax of his quest after God.

Jesus said, "Receive your sight; your faith has saved you." And immediately he received his sight and followed Jesus, glorifying God and all the people when they saw it, gave praise unto God. Your faith has saved you. The word "faith" in the gospels has a much larger meaning than the evangelistic and slightly theological meaning it holds in the popular mind today. The same thing is true of the word "saved." The original Greek, Latin and Anglo-Saxon meaning of the word "save" is to make whole. Salvation is wholeness. We talk about being "saved" today as though it meant subscribing to some religious formula, to some set of doctrine, to some particular church. But when Jesus spoke of salvation, he meant wholeness. When Jesus said, "Your faith has saved you," he had not talked any theology; he had not presented any doctrine. He had brought this man to a condition of wholeness.

Integration is wholeness of mind or personality. An integrated person is a person who is at one within himself and at one with God, and therefore at one with others. This is also the meaning of "salvation." It takes more than medical treatment to cure fundamental dividedness within the patient. Being made whole spiritually prepares the way for miracles on the physical plane.

To go back to Otto Rank again – he enlisted the will of the patient right from the beginning. And I believe that we ought to set ourselves certain objectives – not outlandish ones that we don't feel are reasonably possible. But if you set yourself an objective honestly and sincerely, I believe God will say to you, "Let it be to you according to your faith." A resolution is not something to write in a notebook on the first day of January. A resolution is an effort of the *will.* If you mean business, all your emotional energy, all your mental aptitude, all the cooperation of your friends will combine to give you success in the thing you resolve to do. Faith and will power together are invincible and each supports the other. Your will power strengthens the faith and keeps it in the right direction. And your faith gives energy and potency to your will power.

The most common inhibition from which our wills suffer is that delusion that we are the victims of heredity or environment or some peculiar circumstance. Some of us must go on suffering quite a long time before we discover that the divine will for us and in us is vastly richer and more comfortable than any wish or self-will of our own. No alleged streak of "bad heredity" can hold us down when we affirm that larger will of God.

There is no thing we cannot overcome. Don't say your own evil instinct is inherited, or that one inborn trait makes your whole life forlorn and brings down blame that is not merited.

Behind your parents and grandparents lies the great eternal will. That, too, is your strong, beautiful, divine inheritance: a sure lever of success for one who tries.

"Immediately he regained his sight and followed him, glorifying God, and all the people, when they saw it, praised God." When God opens your eyes, then you can pray for anything. This man is described in the gospels as a blind beggar. We are all blind beggars, aren't we, until our eyes are opened. We beg because we don't see and when our eyes are opened, we don't have to beg. The opening of our eyes is a spiritual process. The opening of our eyes brings the ability to see into the kingdom of heaven, and when we see into the kingdom of heaven, we see the blueprint that God has for each one of us. We are not gambling or betting on the chance that we will be cured in a week. It is nothing like that but what we are really doing is seeking a fuller vision, a vision of the kingdom of God.

When I say, "Your will be done on earth as it is in heaven," I think in terms of the perfect will of God which, relative to us, is in heaven. Heaven is that which is "heaved up." That is the literal meaning of the word in Greek and early English. It is that place which is lifted up above the material and is more true than any material fact. There is a sublime truth, a fundamental and marvelous religious truth in that prayer, "Your will be done on earth as it is in heaven." In other words, this is what it means, "O God, may your perfect blueprint up there be brought down and carried into effect, into action, incarnated in my body, expressed in my mind, registered by my will, acted out by my conduct, in vital faith."

Here is a good meditation to use in connection with this prayer:

> Let me be still. Let me enter into silence.
> I realize that GOD is in the very center of my being.
> Let me remain quiet until I feel God there and know he has charge of all my affairs. Now I have nothing to worry about, for worry implies uncertainty and dividedness, and with God there are no problems, only plans! I was created for the working out of a plan. I commit myself irrevocably to the working out of that plan. Now I am become part of the eternal will of God. So I am at rest and enter into the peace which passes all understanding. Lo, I come to do your will, O my God! O my God, you are true! O my soul, you are happy!
>
> (Pause for Silence).

All of this is very simply written into this beautiful story. When God opens your eyes, you can pray for anything. You will know what to pray for. Receive your sight. Your faith has saved you; your faith has made you whole. It has integrated you – and the rest will follow. Our mission is to bring the healing of Jesus Christ where it will be available to everybody.

> **Let us pray:** Father, we thank you that Jesus Christ is the same yesterday, today and forever. We thank you for the picture which we see in the gospels – the beautiful, technicolor picture– of the Son of Man echoing his Father's will and making that will effective in the lives, bodies, souls and the experience of sick people, poor people, distressed people and frustrated people. May your healing will be accomplished in us. Take our wills and make them yours. Give us grace that our wills may be synchronized with your will, that we may see how marvelous is your perfect will. Open my eyes that I may see the blueprints that you have for me, and then, give me faith to carry them into effect.
>
> May your whole spirit and soul and body be preserved blameless until the coming of Jesus Christ. So it shall be and so it is. Amen.

Questions

1. What is "Will Therapy?"
2. What is the role of the psychologist in helping people get well?
3. Try meditating on the love of God for five minutes. What obstacles and benefits do you find? Try using one of the prayers on page 83-84.

VI

THE CURE OF FEAR

BACK of almost every human problem, whether it be physical, mental, moral, emotional, domestic or economic, there is still another problem, lurking in the background and working in the dark. It is the problem of fear. It has religious, physiological, psychological and practical aspects. Many people know they are suffering from fear. But many people are afraid and don't even realize it. Great authorities have told us that if we could effectually cure fear, we would instantly remove more than fifty per cent of all human distress, physical suffering and disease. If you can get rid of fear, conscious and subconscious, you will have taken a long step on the road to recovery.

At a camp in California several years ago a missionary from China taught us how to sing the chorus "I will not be afraid" in Chinese. She told us that during the war in China the Christian refugees who had lost everything and were threatened with the loss of their lives sang that as a marching song. It had wonderful power to exorcise or cast out fear. It doesn't matter how you get rid of fear, whether you pray it out, sing it out or work it out. But get rid of it! If you can't do it by yourself, get a friend to help you. If you are not afraid yourself, you can actually exercise spiritual healing by being able to sit down or kneel down with a person who is afflicted with chronic fears and help him to dissipate those fears, to get rid of them.

There is a great cathedral in San Francisco that ministers to thousands of people, regardless of denomination. It is one of the glories of the Episcopal Church. But when I visited San Francisco about thirty years ago (probably around 1937), it was just a little chapel. It was built the year after the earthquake. In those days it was not considered good manners in San Francisco to make any reference to the earthquake. It was not discussed. You made no allusions to it. If you had to refer to it, you said "the great fire." But the builders of this cathedral did make a reference to it. They were inspired to do a wonderful work. And in less than a year after the earthquake they started with this little chapel, which was the crypt chapel, the foundation of the whole building. On the little altar there they carved the words, "Though the earth be removed and the mountains be carried into the midst of the sea, we will not fear. God is in the midst of her; she shall not be removed." This was the cure to repressed fear that in those early days animated the minds of many persons in that great city.

Dr. William Sadler wrote some of the most significant books on psychiatry that have ever appeared in print. He gave a marvelous lifetime of service in the field of psychiatry. He practiced in Chicago for about forty years and wrote both popular and technical books in his field. He is a Christian man and back of his psychiatry is a wholesome faith in God. In one of his scholarly books, he has included a chapter on "Religious Therapy." Dr. Sadler says that you must learn to laugh at your fears! Imagine *that* from a man who is a former President of the American College of Surgeons, a former President of the American Psychological Association, and a past President of the Post-Graduate Medical School of Chicago! He says, "Ignore neurotic symptoms! Learn to eradicate your phobias!"[1] People frequently suffer more from physical disorders that they are afraid of than they do from actual physical disorders that have been properly and medically diagnosed.

Dr. Sadler says, "Don't take memory ghosts seriously!" Do you know what a memory ghost is? I do! Because I used to have one! A memory ghost is some trouble, mental or emotional, that came to you per-

---

[1] William S. Sadler, ***Modern Psychiatry*** (St. Louis, Mo.: C. V. Mosby Company).

haps twenty years ago. It is all right now. It does not exist today, but your memory does, and you keep bringing this ghost back into your present consciousness through your memory. You allow that thing that happened twenty years ago to make you unhappy today. The real thing isn't there, but you let its ghost disturb your peace. That is what I did – not for twenty years, but for some time.

It happened in my first parish in Texas when I was a young man, a young Episcopal clergyman. We had Holy Communion every Sunday. One Sunday morning at the early service, I fainted at the altar! There were only about half a dozen people present. It was a trivial thing and it has happened only that once in my life! They took me into the vestry, gave me some water, and in five or ten minutes I was all right. But it hurt my pride that I had fainted at the altar! It isn't done by respectable clergymen! It distressed me greatly! My mind would keep going back to it. I can remember it so well because in the Episcopal Church we have an epistle and a gospel for every Sunday in the Communion service, and I fainted when I was reading the gospel – of all things!

Do you know that that memory ghost played all kinds of tricks with me? For months afterwards every time I would go up to the altar and start reading the gospel, he would walk up to me and say, "Are you going to faint this morning?" Not audibly of course, but through my subconscious. "You know this is where you fainted that Sunday!" And I would have a terrible feeling until I got through the gospel. Then I was all right and could go on through the rest of the service with no trouble. This went on for months. I didn't tell anybody about it. I was ashamed of it.

Then I went for a vacation to Britain and spent some time also in Scotland. The Provost of the Cathedral on the little island of Cumbrae was a priest, a physician and a psychiatrist. He was a medical graduate of the University of Edinburgh. So I told him my story. He didn't make fun of me, but he tried to show me in a logical way how unnecessary it was for me to be held in bondage by that fear. Then we knelt down and prayed, and he cast that fear out of me. I don't know just how he did it but he did it. I was very happy. Then, just as I was leaving the room, he said, "Oh, just a minute! You're celebrating Communion tomorrow morning in the Cathedral." "Yes?" I replied. "All right." Then I added, "You don't mind reading the gospel, do you?" And he said, "WHAT? Why, don't you know the celebrant always reads the Gospel? Don't be foolish! You won't have any difficulty!" And I didn't! And I've never had any difficulty since. Why? Because that memory ghost was cast out. It wasn't there any more.

Seward Hiltner, a minister and a psychologist, has written a book on understanding the self. He has a different phrase for the "memory ghost" Dr. Sadler talks about. Seward Hiltner calls it "*dated emotions*." It is like dated coffee – to assure you that it's fresh! Dated emotions act like this: You were scared. You got into a minor auto wreck about six years ago on the fourth of July. So, since that fourth of July, every time you go for a ride, you think that you are going to have a wreck. That emotion has a history. A book could be written about it. Memory ghosts or *dated emotions* can give us a lot of trouble. They can start fears that go on and on and on, gathering momentum as they go.

There are many forms of religious therapy that will help you to get rid of fear. If you have a prayer group that prays for the healing of people, that is an experiment in religious therapy. If you read such a book as ***The Healing Light*** by Agnes Sanford, the reading of that book for you is religious therapy. If you read any of the pamphlets listed by The International Order of St. Luke the Physician[2] with the idea of get-

---

[2] In the United States: The OSL Resource Center, Order of St. Luke the Physician, PO Box 780909, San Antonio, TX 78278-0909, (877) 992-5222 , (210) 698-7141 local, foreign & fax, oslresourcecenter@satx.rr.com , osl2@satx.rr.com

In Canada: The Churchmouse Resource Centre, A Special Ministry of the Anglican Diocese of Qu'Appelle, 1501 College Avenue, Regina, SK CANADA, S4P1B8, (306) 522-3263, Fax: (306) 352-6808, churchmouse@sasktel.net)

ting help in overcoming adverse conditions or negative conditions of sickness and pain, that is religious therapy. Dr. Sadler says,

> The consoling influence of a fear-free religious experience and the possession of a philosophy of living are both helpful in bringing about emancipation from the slavery of fear, anger, jealousy, worry and revenge. And psychiatry is remiss in that it fails to use these powerful and valuable influences which can be made to contribute to all our efforts to enhance integration of personality and augment the struggle for self-realization.

Then, he continues, "The life of Christ is the consoling influence and his teaching provides the philosophy which makes fear relatively harmless in our lives." In his book, ***Modern Psychiatry***, Dr. Sadler quotes an English authority, Dr. Hyslop, head of one of the oldest and most famous mental hospitals in London. Dr. Hyslop was lecturing on psychiatry before the British Medical Association. In speaking of prayer as a therapeutic agent, he declared,

> As a psychiatrist and one whose life has been concerned with the suffering of the mind, I would state that of all hygienic measures to counteract disturbed sleep,

> depressed spirits, and all the miserable sequels of a distressed mind, I would undoubtedly give first place to the simple habit of prayer.[3]

Though they don't talk much about it, the medical profession is welcoming these superphysical powers, these spiritual forces which we invoke through prayer. Dr. Sadler further quotes these words from Dr. Hyslop in the same address:

> The best medicine my practice has discovered is prayer. The exercise of prayer by those who habitually practice it must be regarded as the most adequate and normal of all pacifiers of the mind and calmers of the nerves.[4]

We see that fear is our great enemy. We must find a cure for it. Doctors recognize this; psychiatrists recognize this; the clergy realize it; so do nurses; so do mothers with sick children; but the question is *HOW*? The first step is to turn to the medicine chest in which the remedies against fear are stored! This is a book on *immateria medica* – the Bible! It has several thousand proved and tried recipes for the defeat of fear and the cure of disease. Most church people know about half a dozen or more good Bible verses. They can use those,

---

[3] Ibid.

[4] Ibid.

but the Bible has thousands of verses that are packed with healing energy, and we should enlarge our knowledge and our spiritual vocabulary through the systematic study and use of the Bible. We ought to have prescriptions from the Bible to meet definite situations. When we talk with a friend or pray with a friend, we ought to know just exactly the right passages to quote out of the Bible and not be limited to the use of a few things that we have memorized, perhaps twenty-five years ago. The Word of God is like a sharp, two-edged sword. You need that sense of having its cutting edge. That makes all the difference. You know how particular a surgeon is to have instruments that are perfectly adjusted for his work and what a terrible job he would make of his work if he did not have just the right instrument at just the right time under just the right conditions.

How may we cure these different fears that we have? We don't all have the same kinds. My answer is: use the words of Jesus first. They are the most potent. Then, use any words in the Bible that are calculated to meet your condition. You will be surprised to find how much specialized material is in the Bible. Now let's consider some specific fears and their remedy.

1. Fear of Danger

This is the most common fear of all and it is really very valuable. Without some fear of danger, we'd be having more wrecks than we do have, and you know that the number of wrecks of all kinds is getting formidable. It has its value and yet, as a fear, it ought not to oppress us. Recall the story of the tempest in the gospels. The disciples were in a little boat on the Sea of Galilee. Jesus was in their midst, but he was asleep. Suddenly a storm came up – one of the little squalls that they have on that lake. And the disciples were almost petrified with fear. "Master, wake up! Master, save us! We are perishing!" they cried. Jesus awakened and what did he say to them? "Oh, you poor things! I realize how much you must be suffering. I'll see if I can do something about it." He did not. He rebuked their fear even before he rebuked the waves. He rebuked the fear inside and then he rebuked the unruly condition outside. He said, "You of little faith, why did you doubt?" Moffatt puts it a little more clearly: "Why are you afraid? How little you trust God!" When you are afraid of danger in that sense, it is a sign of lack of trust in God. To rebuke fear is to enlarge trust. More trust, less fear! More fear, less trust!

2. Fear of Darkness

This is a fear of comparatively few people today because we have such marvelous lighting systems and we don't have the feeling about darkness that our ancestors had. Still there are some people who are afraid of the dark. I know people who can't go to sleep at night unless there is a light in their room or just outside the door so they can see a little. The Bible rebukes the fear of darkness. There are four or five choice prescriptions for this in the Bible. The one I like best is: "I am the light of the world. Whoever follows me will never walk in darkness but will have the light of life." (John 8:12). And then, of course, there are dozens of prescriptions in the Psalms. "You will not fear the terror of the night." (Psalms 91:5). Say that to yourself if there is anything that haunts you at night. It may not be physical darkness that you fear. It may be something that haunts you at bedtime and gives you a feeling of heaviness. Or say this: "Even the darkness is not dark to you; the night is as bright as the day, for darkness is as light to you." (Psalm 139:12)

3. Fear of Poverty

There are people who have an inferiority complex in regard to things, an inadequacy to attract to themselves those desirable and necessary good things of life, and so they develop a fear of poverty. Know your manual of arms for this Christian way of life. Consult your textbook. There is much ammunition against poverty in the Bible. "Therefore I tell you, do not worry about your life, what you will eat, what you will drink, or about your body, what you will wear. For it is the Gentiles (the unbelievers) who strive for these things. Strive first for the kingdom of God and his righteousness and all these things will be given to you as well." "Fear not, little flock," says Jesus, "It is the Father's good pleasure to give you the kingdom." Any suggestion of poverty there? Any suggestion of bankruptcy there? Any suggestion of lack of resources there? "All things are yours and you are Christ's and Christ is God's." There is a string to that one! When you can say you "are Christ's," then you can say, "all things" are yours. But you can't say all things "are yours" until you first postulate that other line, that you "are Christ's"!

4. Fear of Physical Crisis

This might take the form of fear of an impending illness. You know there are some people who say, "I feel an illness coming on." There is fear behind that remark. They are going to bring it on if they feel that way! Or they have been told by their doctor that they might need a surgical operation. That fills them with dread. It might be a very simple operation. Circumstances being what they are, the complexity of life, their own background, their physical condition may demand a little surgery. We are all different. I am not a perfectionist. I do not say if you believe in God you will never need a doctor or medicine. God is no respecter of persons, but a respecter of conditions. If we respect the conditions, then God gets through and does marvelous things for us. There are some magnificent verses in the Bible for those who face physical crises. The fear of physical crises is nearly always very much worse than the crises themselves. It is the fear that makes them so dreadful. That word "dreadful" means "full of dread." The only way to lick this fear is to be filled with some other emotion that ousts the dread and gives you a mind at peace with yourself and God. "God will keep you in perfect peace when you keep your mind centered on him because you trust him."

There are physical crises which are not pathological. Childbirth is a good example. Thousands of women, facing the prospect of childbirth, know it is a natural thing, and yet they dread it. They have been told by their friends what terrible things can happen, or they have read about things that have happened at childbirth and so, instead of looking forward to it with great joy as Mary did in the Bible, they look forward to it with great dread. It is a physical crisis which inspires them with fear. Any Christian ought to be able to sit down with a prospective mother and talk with her simply and convincingly about the power of God to take away that fear. There should not be this fear, but when there is, you must respect it – or at least you must respect the person having it. Recall the first chapter of the Gospel of Luke. Even Mary, who was perhaps one of the most perfect characters of whom we have any record, was filled with fear when she first found she was going to have a baby. We don't like to think of any faults whatever in the character of the Virgin Mary, but, nevertheless, she was inspired by a natural fear when she heard that she was to have a baby. God sent an archangel, Gabriel, to her to tell her of her destiny and to rebuke her fear. He says, "Do not be afraid, Mary. The Holy Spirit will come upon you and the power of the Most High will overshadow you, therefore, the child to be born will be holy; he will be called the Son of God." If you will change the word "Son" to a little "s" instead of a big "S," you can say that to any prospective mother. Tell her that the child that God will give her shall be called a child of God. Every baby born is a Word of God incarnate, a word that is in process of being made flesh, and the sooner we understand that, the better for our mothers and the better for our families and the better for our future prospects. Help her to get the joy of that and the joy will blot out all fear.

5. Fear of Enemies

As I travel around the country today I see, even among college graduates, highly intelligent and well-informed people and people with Christian backgrounds, a terrible fear of war. Much of our inflation is due, I think, to the fear of war. Our rather unfortunate and compromising relationship with certain other countries in Europe and Asia is due to fear of war. Because we are afraid of a third world war, our businessmen, politicians, and alleged statesmen sow the seeds of fear. The fear in their own minds becomes projected into their speeches and writings. The newspapers catch it; the radios catch it. It is a sort of epidemic of fear of war, and it circulates all over the country. We have to learn to use the antidote to the fear of war. It is not enough to bolster up our courage by a lot of pious talk. But if we have faith in God, a real faith, if we have learned from Jesus how to have faith in God, we shall not be afraid of World War III.

If you are afraid of World War III and want to find out from the Bible how a military situation can be controlled by prayer, you will find such a story dramatically told in 2 Kings 6. It is an amazing story, a story of Elisha. A little town in Palestine, the town of Dothan, was under attack. The Syrian army outnumbered the Israelite army by nine to one. Wouldn't you be afraid if your army was surrounded by an enemy army nine times as strong numerically? Many of the leaders of Israel were afraid, but there was one man of clear vision and thought. It was the prophet Elisha and he was there in the town. His servant came in and announced the sudden attack. Elisha was perfectly calm and cool. He knew he didn't have to be afraid. The servant didn't know it. He said, "Oh, my lord, what shall we do?" Elisha looked at the young man and said, "Don't be afraid." Why? When the Bible says, "Don't be afraid," there is always a reason. "Don't be afraid," said Elisha, "for those who are with us are more than those who are with them." Where was Elisha's arithmetic? Didn't he know that the enemy was nine times as strong as the little home army? Then Elisha prayed, saying, "O Lord, open his eyes that he may see." And the Lord did open the young man's eyes and he saw chariots and horsemen round about Elisha. Reinforcements? Yes, but not the usual military type! They were celestial forces, probably a legion of angels. I believe in angels. The Bible teaches the reality of angels. They are not apparitions, or ghosts. They are real. They are under the control of God and the Holy Spirit. You don't have to be afraid if you are on God's side! Don't pray to God to be on your side. Pray that you may be on his side.

The army of Syria was defeated without the shedding of a drop of blood. They were taken captive and marched into the city under the spell of psychic blindness. Then the King of Israel said to Elisha, "Shall I kill them?" We can imagine Elisha smiling as he answered, "No, don't kill them! Feed them!" A great deal of war in the world today can be traced to the lack of food. When people are hungry, you can stir up all kinds of strife, rebellion, warfare, jealousy, hatred and antagonism. So, they didn't kill them. They fed them. And the armies of Syria no longer came to disturb Israel. There are many strange and wonderful things in this chapter, an anticipation and experience of laws that we are only now beginning to understand. It is well worth study. You can catch a glimpse of telepathy, television, radar control, and extrasensory perception! That chapter is a beautiful answer to the fear of war.

6. Fear of Death

"The last enemy that will be destroyed is death." You destroy death by destroying the fear of death. It is the fear of death that hurts. Death has no objective existence; it is a transition. But the fear of death is dreadful. Jesus overcame death, not for himself alone but for all of us. The resurrection was not a stunt performed by the Son of God. It was a foretaste of the destiny of all Christ's people, perhaps eventually of all mankind. I don't think Jesus will overcome death. I think he *has* overcome death. Prayer to overcome the fear of death will simply give you your proper share in the complete victory that Christ has already achieved.

Jesus said, "Whoever keeps my Word will never taste death." (John 8:51). I take those words at their face value. I do not think Jesus was speaking in parables. I think he meant just what he said. What is full of dread and terror to the unregenerate person, the person who is not consciously "in Christ," becomes just a pleasant journey to those who are "in Christ." What we call death is just "transition" for those whose eyes have been opened spiritually. We are never to see death. In consciousness, we shall never know that there is such a thing! I remember a dear friend of mine who died rather early in life – at the age of sixty. Everybody expected him to live to be eighty! He was tired one night and went to bed early. In the morning they found that his spirit had gone. A smile still flickered on his face. The doctor said it was due to heart trouble. That was all he could say. Actually he had made the transition without even knowing it. Two doctor friends of mine have told me out of their own medical experience that the majority of their patients do not see death. The spirit goes an hour, sometimes two hours, before the body dies. Your body is not you. You possess a body as long as you live in it. When Jesus said, "Whoever keeps my Word will never taste death," he was not saying something irrational or illogical, even according to practical observation. Death is the final demonstration of victory for us as Christians. "Even though I walk through the darkest valley," said the Psalmist, " I fear no evil; for you are with me." I wish we did not keep these words primarily for funeral services. We say some beautiful things at funerals that ought to be said about twenty years before the person dies. There is another magnificent saying which ought not to be kept for funeral oratory. It ought to be said when we are well and strong and have no thought of disease or death: From John 11:25-26, "I am the resurrection and the life." I AM! Not "I will be" but I AM! "Those who believe in me, even though they die, will live, and everyone who lives and believes in me will never die." If we really believe those words, we cannot tolerate any fear of death.

The secret of overcoming fear is to practice the presence of God. "I fear no evil." Why? "For you are with me." All our fears are fears of evil of some kind. If you have caught this perspective, you can say as truthfully as the psalmist said, "Even though I walk through the darkest valley, I fear no evil; for you are with me." "For I am persuaded that neither death, nor life, nor angels, nor principalities, nor powers, nor things present, nor things to come, nor height, nor depth, nor any other creature, shall be able to separate us from the love of God which is in Christ Jesus our Lord."

> **Let us pray:** Dear Lord Jesus, We thank you for your complete triumph over fear. We thank you that your victory over fear is ours also and we take it! We

know that all is well because you are with us, your presence follows us. Nothing can separate us from the love of God in Jesus Christ. May every fear as it rises be quieted and dismissed through the glorious knowledge of your presence. Help us to dwell in the secret place of the most high and to abide under the shadow of the Almighty, for the kingdom and the power and the glory are yours for ever and ever. Amen.

Questions

1. Write down your memory ghosts.
2. What have you done to get rid of them?
3. What methods are suggested? List (underline or highlight) the fears and the help for each one that is suggested? What other suggestions do you have?

VII

THE CURE OF OBSESSIONS

Then he returned from the region of Tyre, and went by way of Sidon towards the Sea of Galilee, in the region of the Decapolis. They brought to him a deaf man who had an impediment in his speech; and they begged him to lay his hand on him. He took him aside in private, away from the crowd, and put his fingers into his ears, and he spat and touched his tongue. Then looking up to heaven, he sighed and said to him, "Ephphatha," that is "Be opened." And immediately his ears were opened, his tongue was released, and he spoke plainly. Then Jesus ordered them to tell no one; but the more he ordered them, the more zealously they proclaimed it. They were astounded beyond measure, saying, "He has done everything well; he even makes the deaf to hear and the mute to speak.

– Mark 7:31-37

> Now he was casting out a demon that was mute; when the demon had gone out, the one who had been mute spoke, and the crowds were amazed. But some of them said, "He casts out demons by Beelzebul, the ruler of the demons." Others, to test him, kept demanding from him a sign from heaven. But he knew what they were thinking and said to them, "Every kingdom divided against itself becomes a desert, and house falls on house. If Satan is divided against himself, how will his kingdom stand? For you say that I cast out the demons by Beelzebul. Now if I cast out the demons by Beelzebul, by whom do your exorcists cast them out? Therefore they will be your judges. But if it is by the finger of God that I cast out the demons, then the kingdom of God has come to you. When a strong man, fully armed, guards his castle, his property is safe.
>
> – Luke 11:14-21

Jesus healing the sick and casting out demons are two aspects of the same phenomenon. The same Jesus who cured blindness and paralysis also cured mental obsessions and those who were emotionally unbalanced. The above story related by Mark and Luke is a little treasury of gospel history. In the one record the man is referred to as having a "demon of muteness" and you can form your own conjecture as to the nature of the obsession. In the other story, he is not described as being demonized, but simply as having an impediment in his speech and being deaf. It is very interesting.

There is vastly more in this story than a casual reading will reveal. There is dynamite in it. I've learned to read the gospels with a sort of fourth-dimensional faculty. What do I mean by that? I mean that I try to transcend the limitations of time and space. I have read them over and over in Greek and other languages, and I am familiar with the historical narrative. But when I read them in a fourth-dimensional way, the limitations of time and space vanish and, instead of happening nineteen hundred years ago, they are happening now, right before my eyes. Instead of happening in Palestine they are happening here– where I am, where you are! It takes a little practice. But the more you do it, the easier it gets. Learn to interpret these glorious miracles as contemporary demonstrations of God's love and power. You can read them that way when you are all alone in your own room. With the eyes of your soul, with your spiritual vision, you can recapture a story like this, and it can be brought right into the present moment. You might be like one of the disciples, watching it. Or if you are in need of healing, you might take the character of the person who is healed and learn how to put yourself into a position for the great physician to work on you. So, learn to transcend time and space when you read the gospels!

The Word of God is a living word. There is an incredible power that defies our definition in the pages of these four gospels. No matter how often they are read, one always finds them fresh and sees new light streaming from them.

It is worthwhile analyzing a story like this, not just intellectually, but seeing it as a slow motion picture. Familiarity breeds contempt. We think we know these stories. When the minister reads them Sunday morning at eleven o'clock, we think, "that's a very beautiful story. I've read it many times; I know it." Do you? Are you sure? Would you know what to tell a man with a mute spirit if you met him downtown? Would you? What would you tell him? Would you tell him he ought to read this story in the gospel? He wouldn't do it! If he did, he wouldn't know what to do about it! Could you instruct a man with a mute spirit to the point that he would lose his mute spirit? If you can, then you know the story. If you can't, you don't know this story. You know a little bit about it. I am not being severe! I want you to see that even the best of us need a deeper penetration into the divine truth in these miracles.

What is a miracle? If that question were put to a group of Christian people, many different answers might be given. Is a miracle something that defies our credulity? Is a miracle something that goes beyond reason? Is it something that reverses all the known laws of science? Not necessarily! In the New Testament, there are at least three different words for miracles, used in the Greek. There is *teras* – a wonder, a portent. There is *semeion* – a sign, sometimes translated "miracle." Then, there is that word *dunamis* – a work of power. *Dunamis* is the Greek word from which we get our English word "dynamic" or "dynamo." That is the word I like best. In the miracles of Jesus there is an incredible, an almost indefinable power which he could release at will. He could release it in the person with whom he was working. He could evoke it from the very soul and life of the patient. We haven't investigated this to anything like the degree that medical doctors and psychiatrists investigate the recuperative capacity of human nature. We've been content to say, "Oh, yes, of course I believe in the miracles. The miracles were given to show that Jesus was the Son of God." Oh? You mean back in the first century? Well, I want something that will prove that Jesus is the Son of God this year in my city! In your city! It is not enough for me that a sign was given nineteen centuries ago to prove that Jesus was the Son of God, but I want something to prove that he is the Son of God right now! *Dunamis* is the word! Of course, there will be people who will interpret these things as *terrata*, portents, wonders, supernormal demonstrations, but I want this *dunamis*, this work of power!

Now, when you see this story as a slow-motion picture, what do you find Jesus doing? You find him doing just what you would like to have done. I am not being irreverent. Jesus showed extraordinarily good judgment in the handling of this man– such judgment as we would like to be able to show if we knew how. Those who brought this man to Jesus suggested that perhaps he would like to put his hands upon him. Well, as a matter of fact, Jesus didn't do it. He didn't always do what people said he ought to do. Watch the slow-motion picture! What did he do?

The man was suffering from a sense of inferiority – naturally – for he had an impediment in his speech. This was so painfully evident that the people thought he had a mute spirit. Maybe he did in one sense of the word! His affliction had made him supernormally shy. He didn't like to be around people. People didn't understand him, he thought, and he didn't always understand them. He met Jesus in a little town. Jesus saw that he was afraid of the crowd. Did Jesus say, "Clench your fists! Keep a stiff upper lip! Just stay right here in the crowd!" He did not. Jesus did the kind thing, the courteous thing. The first thing he did was to take the man away from the crowd. The crowd bothered him. The crowd distracted him. The crowd made it almost impossible for the man to exercise any real act of faith. Jesus just took him by the hand and led him out of the crowd, out of the town, maybe out into a country lane.

But the man was deaf. Jesus knew that. Did Jesus say, "Just forget about that! That's just an error of mortal mind!" He did not. Jesus used what any kind, thoughtful person will use for a deaf person. He used the sign language. He used a language that this man would understand. He touched his tongue. He put his fingers into the man's ears. Why? To suggest to the man in a gentle, persuasive, convincing way that he could have his hearing restored and that be could have his impediment removed. We need a lot of understanding in dealing with sick people. Not sympathy in the sentimental sense, but understanding. Jesus understood what was in the man. He had that great gift of intuitional diagnosis.

My common sense tells me and my faith tells me and my love of Christ tells me that we ought to be able to handle some of these cases the way Jesus handles them. We ought to stop that foolish and rather skeptical alibi that these things only belong in the first century. It is high time we took them out of the first century and demonstrated them as part of the phenomena of modern Christianity.

I went to a school thirty-two years ago in Missouri where I studied therapeutic psychology. The head of the school was a very beautiful Christian character and he put a great deal of understanding, Christian teaching into his psychology. I've never met anybody like him since that time. He had had some wonderful cures in his own work. He had a sanitarium where he carried out his teaching. The sanitarium was under his medical supervision but he used psychological techniques chiefly. He had a beautiful Christian spirit. Sidney Weltmer used to take some of his students aside and give them a little private instruction. He would tell them about his own work, not egotistically, but just to show them what could be done. I remember one day when he had a few students around, and we had begun to understand his secret and to glow with enthusiasm, he said these remarkable words, "You can do what I do when you know what I know and I can teach you what I know." He had been telling us about some remarkable healings that seemed almost like miracles, though they were not in the strict sense. Then – "You can do what I do when you know what I know and I can teach you what I know." Does that suggest to you a certain famous remark of Jesus', "The works that I do you will also do and greater works than these will you do." Does the modern Church believe that? Should anybody attempt to do the work that Jesus did, he would very likely be regarded as a charlatan! Did Jesus mean what he said? I think he did. I think it is our business to learn how Jesus functioned, to learn how he did his miracles, to investigate them reverently, lovingly, but also with the highest mental capacity which we can bring to bear upon them. I believe that in certain parts of the world all the miracles of Jesus are being duplicated today and some greater miracles are actually being wrought. I get some remarkable stories sent to me from all parts of the world and I'm not talking superficially when I say this. Is this story that we have been considering so unreasonable?

Jesus took the man aside. He used the sign language. He touched his ears. He touched his tongue. He anointed his tongue with saliva – very disgusting to our modern ideas, but quite a normal procedure in an Oriental country. Saliva was regarded as having great therapeutic power.

And then Jesus looked up to heaven. The man still had not received his hearing. He was still watching Jesus. He was using the powers he possessed to get into rapport with this wonderful person. When Jesus looked up to heaven, the man looked up too. He looked up, and as he looked away from himself, things began to happen. That is true for all of our sick people. All of you, who seek healing, remember that your healing begins when you look away from yourself. Your healing is retarded immeasurably by self-contemplation, by self-pity – "Why doesn't somebody pay me a little attention? Why aren't people kinder to me? Why does not somebody do something for me?" That doesn't get you anywhere in spiritual healing. It is when we get to the point of looking away from ourselves that we are ready for the voice of God to speak to us. There is possibly a detachment even for a sick person, yes, even for a mentally sick person, even for an emotionally sick person. So, he looked up to heaven. Jesus looks and the man follows his gaze, and then Jesus knows by this faculty of intuitional diagnosis, that the man is ready, the conditions are right. Five or ten minutes ago they were not, but they are now, and Jesus is very economical of time. He takes his time, but he doesn't take a minute extra. Now, the man is ready! Now, Jesus speaks audibly. Hitherto he had only spoken in sign language. Now he says, "*Ephphatha*," – that is "Be opened!" And then the miracle happens. His ears were opened and "the bond of his tongue was loosed." The bond is the "string" of his tongue as translated in the King James version. You can feel that there is a string back in your mouth that holds the tongue in place. This man was under incredible tension and this string had been taut. The other story says that the man had a mute demon.

There are many people who are not mute in a literal sense. They can speak audibly and clearly but they are "mute" spiritually. They have capacities for self-expression, but their ability to express what God has given them to say or to be or to do is almost totally inhibited. Many of the inhibitions that you read about in books on popular psychology are really muteness – that is failure to express what God has breathed into you to say. Your life should say something, not just your lips, but your life, your vocation, your witness before the world. You ought to say something that God wants spoken. There is an old prayer in the Prayer Book with words to the effect that we should show forth in our lives what we say with our lips. Words are not enough. They need a life to back them up. Jesus restored a lost faculty to this man. There was no disease there. A careful examination would have found nothing except extreme tension, but a modern psychiatrist would have discovered that this man was petrified by inhibitions. He had this condition which the Bible describes with the Greek word *kophos*. The evil spirit is the spirit which holds him in bondage. He is not free, but Jesus comes to release him. "And immediately his ears were opened, his tongue was released, and he spoke plainly. Then Jesus ordered them to tell no one (but that was more than you could expect!); but the more he ordered them, the more zealously they proclaimed it. They were astounded beyond measure, saying, "He has done everything well; he even makes the deaf to hear and the mute to speak."

There is a great deal of nonsense spread abroad about evil spirits. There is much ignorance in the Church concerning "demonization," yet some most interesting books have been written about it. A man by the name of McCasland[1] has written a very good book in which he actually, perhaps for the first time, intelligently discriminates between psychological disease like phobias, schizophrenia, neuroses and psychoses on the one hand, and actual demonization on the other. The author shows in his book that there are some cases where you can classify them either way. For instance, he shows how, in a modern compulsion neurosis, which is a mental disease well understood by psychiatrists, you have what in Jesus' day would have been called demonization. But the important thing, as this author points out, is that these symptoms, which are so easily diagnosed today but which are with such great difficulty cured, Jesus was able to heal. Jesus is still equal to the situation. We can still use the technique of Jesus to cast out evil, to overcome evil with good. One of Jesus' most glorious state-

[1] The book referred to in this chapter is ***By The Finger of God***, by S. Vernon McCasland, D. D. It deals with Demon Possession and Exorcism in Early Christianity in the Light of Modern Views of Mental Illness. Macmillan.

ments is, "But if it is by the finger of God that I cast out demons, then the kingdom of God has come to you." (Luke 11:20).

That is one of the most powerful things said by Jesus about his own work of exorcism. And if the kingdom of God has come near to you, then you can cast out evil. Many of you know of Agnes Sanford. She was born in the mission field. Her mother and father were missionaries. She married the son of a missionary, Edgar Sanford, whose parents were missionaries in China. Agnes Sanford's brother lent me a book that his father had written on demonization based on actual cases in the mission field of China. These cases are very familiar on the mission field, more so than here at home. They are not uncanny; they are phenomena of all times which need to be better understood.

What did Jesus teach about demonization? Several things:

1. Demonization made the victim abnormal in health and conduct. Jesus destroyed the cause of the trouble and the symptoms disappeared.

2. For reasons that seemed good to him, Jesus directly addressed the obsessing influence. He did not usually address the patient. A modern psychologist would say, "Yes, but we know now that the devil was really part of the patient's own nature!" All right. It was a split part of the patient's personality. Jesus ad-

dressed the influence whatever it was. He did not rebuke the patient. He rebuked the obsessing influence.

3. Jesus did not argue with the evil spirit. And you'd better not either!

I've done a little work in mental hospitals, not a great deal but enough to know the futility of ever arguing with a mental patient. A mental illness, of course, does not necessarily mean "demonization." Mental disorders, as such, are not demonization. Yet there are people in nearly every mental hospital who are demonized, but the majority of mental disorders are not in this class.

Let me give you an example. I was called several years ago by a clergyman friend of mine whom I had known for years. I knew his wife very well also. He said, "Elizabeth is in a mental hospital in Chicago, and if you are in that part of the country, won't you please try to stop in and see her?" I didn't know too much about such cases and I wasn't too eager to do it – but they were old friends. I had known this woman when she was perfectly normal so I thought perhaps I would be a good person to go and see her. I would go to see her and I would go to see her as though she were the person I remembered many years previously when I was a minister in her state.

I went to the hospital and saw the superintendent first. He said, "Why, you're just the right person! You will do her more good than we can possibly do her!" That was encouraging. Then he sent for an attendant and the attendant took me into her room, and there was Elizabeth! He locked the door and said, "I'll be back in half an hour."

I spoke briefly with Elizabeth, told her I was glad to see her, which was perfectly true, and chatted with her about old times for four or five minutes. Then I said, "Now, Elizabeth, what's the trouble? We've only just got so much time. Let's use it! George sent me to see you and I'm glad to come, if only for old times' sake. What is the trouble?"

"Oh," she said, "Gayner, I have a devil. I am possessed with a devil!

"Why," I said, "You don't look like it."

"Oh," she said, "But I am!"

I asked, "What's the trouble? How does this devil affect you or afflict you?"

"This devil makes me commit the unpardonable sin," she replied. That didn't impress me because I knew enough about mental hospitals to know that in nearly every one of them you visit there are at least two or three people who claim that they have committed the unpardonable sin. You don't take that seriously. So I asked, "Are you sure it's a devil?"

"Oh yes, I'm sure it's a devil." Now, of course, then I was tempted to argue the point, but I had learned that little bit of wisdom that you do not argue with a mental patient. It is utterly futile to do so. The more you argue with them, the more they will rejoice in the opportunity to keep up their end of the argument. You won't get anywhere. So I thought of what Jesus did. He agreed with them. I agreed with her. "All right, then; it is a devil." Then, I said, "Elizabeth, you have read the Bible! Now, then, what did Jesus do with people who were possessed with demons? Come on, now. A direct answer! What did Jesus do with people who were possessed with a devil?"

She looked at me, and said, "Why, of course, Jesus cast out the devil, didn't he?"

"He certainly did," I answered, and continued, "Don't you think he can do the same for you?"

She fixed her eyes on me and said, "Oh, could he?"

"Why, he not only could," I replied, "But he sent me for that very purpose. That is why he sent me to see you, Elizabeth."

She was very much interested. "Do you really believe that?" she asked.

"Of course I do," I answered. "Elizabeth, are you willing to pray with me that God will cast out this devil from you?"

And she said, "Yes indeed, I am." She seemed to be perfectly normal, perfectly sane, for that part of our conversation.

I said, "All right. Let's kneel down!" We knelt down together in that bare room and I just prayed in a very few words that God would cast out this obsession whatever it was, and she would never again be afflicted with it. Then, I used the very words of Jesus, "Thou evil spirit, come out of her and never enter again into her and never trouble her anymore." And immediately, like a flash, she burst into a paroxysm of weeping. Even that did not surprise me because I know that it is a normal reaction under those conditions. I just let her weep. She wept and wept – a veritable outburst – as though she were weeping something out of her whole system. When the weeping let up, I said, "Now, then, let's thank God this thing is gone.

She asked, "Has it?"

"It certainly has," I answered. "Don't you feel it is gone?"

"Yes, I do!" And it had! In less than three weeks she was home with her husband.

Now, there are those who may say, "That was an easy case – very elementary." All right, it was an elementary case. But it yielded to the simple technique of Jesus. When we have the courage, or the faith, or whatever you call it, the perseverance, the tenacity of purpose to tackle these cases in the power of Jesus, in the spirit of Jesus, by the method of Jesus, we are not going to have any trouble. I did not have to struggle with her. It was an easy case. It was just a matter of facing it in the Spirit of Jesus, and letting him do the work.

I've had other cases, not as easy. They always terrify me a little at first. I never want to take up these cases. You know, the early Church had exorcists. The casting out of demons is generally known as exorcism. In the early Church – in the second, third and fourth centuries – when a man told the leaders of the Church that he was called to the ministry, he was expected to show that he could heal the sick and cast out demons. For many years the Church had exorcists as a minor order of its ministry. That was not idle superstition. We would be very much better off and our mental hospitals would be much less crowded today if we had a practical ministry of exorcism in our Christian churches.

I was in Oxford attending two conferences some years ago and I had a free day between the two. I was staying at one of the Oxford colleges. I don't know how these people found out that I was there, but a young married woman came in with her mother to see me. She said, "Will you pray for my mother?" I had never seen them before. I did not know who they were but, of course, when you are asked to pray for a person, the only answer is "yes." I wasn't supposed to be on duty at all, but you are always on duty when people need you. I did not know what the trouble was.

I looked at the mother and said, "Would you like me to pray for you? Your daughter has requested it, but I don't feel that I want to unless you want it."

And to my amazement the older woman said, "No, I don't!"

I asked, "You mean you came with your daughter, your daughter wants prayer for you, and you don't want it?" The woman had a sort of vacant look, and I could not understand it.

I turned to the daughter and said, "What is the trouble with your mother?"

The younger woman was almost in tears. "She's in great trouble," she answered. "I wish you would pray with her."

To which I replied, "I'm sorry, but it is no good praying with her unless she is willing to pray. I just don't think it is right to insist on praying with her when she does not seem to want to pray. But I'll be here tomorrow and if she feels more inclined, bring her back again tomorrow and we will have prayer." So they went away.

The next day about the same time back they came. "Well, how about it?" I asked the daughter. "Does your mother want to have prayer now?"

"Won't you please ask her?" she said.

I turned to the older woman and inquired, "Would you like to have prayer?" And the oddest look, such as I had never seen before, came over the older woman's face as she said, "NO, I DON'T WANT PRAYER!" And then, without any warning, she burst into the most terrible stream of blasphemy, such as I had never heard before. Then I knew what the trouble was. I looked right into her eyes and held up my hand and said, "You cannot talk like that here! Furthermore, you are not speaking those words, but the evil spirit in you is speaking those words. And in the name of Jesus Christ, I command that evil spirit come out of you!" I said it in no uncertain terms. If you do this at all, you have to be very positive. It is utterly useless otherwise. But you are not speaking in your own name. You are speaking in the name of Jesus. The woman passed out and we had to help her onto a sofa. This lasted for two or three minutes.

The daughter was very much concerned, but I said, "Don't worry! Your mother is better already. You see the very power of the thing has passed. That is why she is resting in this faint. She will be all right." She was. We gave her some water and she came around in a few minutes and said, "Now, won't you pray for me?"

And with a totally different look on her face, she joined us in prayer and in thanksgiving.

A psychiatrist might say, "A very simple case! Nothing much to that!" All right! But what do you do when you meet people like that? Do you know how to handle them as Jesus did? Do you know how to use the technique of Jesus? You should. Any disciple should be able to do that. You don't need a minister for that. A Christian layman or laywoman could do just that. Nobody ever told me how to do these things or trained me in the doing of them. I just read about them in the Bible. I was foolish enough to imagine that the Bible really meant what it said. I still think it does. If we take the Bible at its face value and do the things that Jesus did and told his disciples to do, we will get results too. We must pray for a right judgment in all things so that we may quickly recognize the needs of people to whom we minister.

You will recall the tenth chapter of the Gospel of Luke. It tells the story of the seventy who were sent out. Jesus sent them out two by two to preach the Gospel and declare the kingdom of God. He said, "Whenever you enter a town and people welcome you, eat what is set before you, cure the sick who are there, and say to them, 'the kingdom of God is come near to you.'" History is repeating itself today. Where men and women are willing to accept the commission that Jesus gives, the power of Jesus is back of their work. They don't have to work on their own initiative. There are people today who can say, "Lord, in your name even the demons submit to us." I could tell you other stories, but there is no need.

We need the disciplines of Jesus. We need the disciplines of the Church also insofar as they conform to the pattern of Jesus. But we need the discipline of Jesus, those he himself taught. We need degrees of initiation beyond those which we have already achieved. There are further degrees in the Christian faith beyond those which the average church member has ever achieved. We are too ready to assume that we have reached a certain standard of perfection because we have joined the church, we are regular contributors and regular communicants. I wish we could say that every communicant is ready to take up the whole program of Jesus for the redemption of the world today. Healing is an indispensable part of the gospel of redemption.

But let us look further at Jesus' teaching about demonization. We have seen that demonization made the victim abnormal in health and conduct and that Jesus destroyed the cause of the trouble, and the symptoms then disappeared. We have seen that Jesus addressed and rebuked the obsessing influence. He did not rebuke the patient. And we have seen that Jesus did not argue with the evil spirit.

4. Jesus exorcised "by the finger of God" and by the affirming of God's kingdom (see Luke 11:20). This suggests the apostolic exhortation to "overcome evil with good," and is a powerful piece of evidence that it is undoubtedly God's revealed purpose that evil should be annihilated by the declaration of his omnipotence. The terms "finger of God" and "kingdom

of God," used together in this verse, are evidences of this revealed purpose which becomes effective through Jesus.

5. Jesus commanded his followers to exorcise in his name. A survey of the verses in which this authority is given makes it clear that exorcism is far more than any mere incantation or muttered formula. It is an invocation and release of the power of the Spirit to banish an adverse or malicious condition.

6. This power can be exercised only in a spirit of prayer and humility. History shows that exorcism has been practiced successfully (following our Lord's example) only by those who have lived near to the Lord and who have become quick channels for the influence of the Holy Spirit.

The urge and motive of the clergy will not be so much to study and practice "exorcism" as such. Rather they will seek to fulfill their ordination vows and make themselves "faithful dispensers" of the Word of God and of his holy sacraments! This will always include (more or less) a ministry in healing and exorcism.

"These signs will accompany those who believe..."

The Reverend W. Fred Allen writes out of a most intelligently consecrated experience as follows:

> Beneath the irrationality, confusion of mind, and distorted ideas, the spirit of

> the man is intact and suffering only from alienation from God, whether willful or otherwise, and can be reached, ministered to, and healed without the ordering of the mind itself, and the mind itself is vastly helped by the reactions of the spirit and in many cases entirely cured.
>
> Spiritual qualities survive when mental are dead. We reach the spirit through the subconscious when the mind is partly intact; through the spirit direct, by the sacraments, when there is no mentality, only love and desire... It is manifest that the health of the spirit means always help, and sometimes entire cure for the mind.

One can scarcely realize the tremendous power of suggestion. Through the proper use of it, the spirit of the patient may be converted from a powerhouse of hate to a powerhouse of love. In obsessed cases, the patient is possessed by suggestions to consciousness not in conformity with the rational universe, with the truth or with reality. He is possessed by an untruth. That must be driven out by a stronger and more powerful suggestion which will bring to the patient's subconscious mind an intuition of truth. We cannot argue with the possessed that God exists and will help them, but we can suggest this positively and overwhelmingly. Some years ago John Rathbone Oliver said that if we have a keen, bright faith in God, our faith will get over and lighten those in the dim land of shadows.

> **Let us pray:** O God, open our eyes and our hearts and take away our slowness to perceive. Put your fingers into our ears, touch our tongues, say to us the word, "*Ephphatha*, Be opened!" And may our capacity to speak your words be restored to us, and especially bless those who come to you with any great need:
>
> O Saviour Christ, our woes dispel;
> For some are sick, and some are sad,
> And some have never loved Thee well
> And some have lost the love they had.
>
> And none, O Lord, have perfect rest,
> For none are wholly free from sin;
> And those who fain would love Thee best
> Are conscious most of wrong within.
>
> Thy touch has still its ancient power;
> No word from thee can fruitless fall;
> Hear, in this solemn evening hour,
> And in Thy mercy heal us all. Amen.

Questions

1. Read Mark 1:21-28 and Luke 4:31-37, the man with the unclean spirit, and Matthew 9:32, the mute who was demonized, and Matthew 12:22 and Luke 11: 14, the man who was blind, could not speak, and was demonized. What is Jesus' method of healing in each case?

2. Banks lists six steps in the cure of obsession and/or "the casting out of demons." Read each step and think about what that means today. Another step that is practiced today is that before anything of this type is practiced, the person asks for the protection of the Holy Spirit, and is in prayer and quite often, fasting.

3. If you knew a person who seemed to be demonized, how could God help this person through you?

VIII

THE POWER OF FAITH

How to Acquire the Faith Which Brings Healing

> Jesus said unto him, "If you are able!– All things can be done for the one who believes."
>
> – Mark 9:23

Context: The disciples have failed to bring healing to an epileptic child and are now perplexed. So they bring the child and his father to Jesus. At this very moment the child has another seizure. Jesus talks with the father, and the father at last exclaims: "If you can do anything, do help us, do have pity on us." Jesus said to him, "If you can! Anything can be done for one who believes!" At once the father of the boy cried out, "I do believe; help my unbelief!"[1] (Mark 9:22–24)

---

[1] From *The Bible -A New Translation* by James Moffatt. Copyright 1922-1935 and 1950 by Harper & Brothers. Used by permission.

Another translation

> The father said: "If there is anything you can do, take pity on us and help us!" Jesus said to him, "If there is anything I can do! Everything is possible for one who has faith!" The boy's father immediately cried out, "I have faith! Help my lack of faith!"[2]

THE OBJECT of this lesson is: first, to arrive at clearer understanding of the meaning of faith; second, to see how faith accelerates the process of healing; and third, to increase our own faith. Nothing will bring success in this quest so rapidly as the frequent study of the gospel miracles, not a cursory reading, but deep, prayerful, persevering study of these records. If you read these with any normal degree of imagination, you can hardly fail to grasp this basic idea of faith – where it comes from, how it works, how it may be multiplied or stimulated, or even communicated from one person to another.

How do we actually use the imagination here? Surely by seeing the story enacted before our eyes – just as you would watch a television show. As you watch your TV you know there are no real people on your set, but you also know there are images, or reflections,

---

[2] Goodspeed, Edgar J., ***The New Testament: An American Translation.***

of real people there. Imagination is just the making of these mental images which represent actual people. When you learn to cultivate this power of imagination, or visualization, you can identify yourself with the person in the story who comes to Jesus for healing. You can do this whether the patient happens to be yourself or some other person for whom you seek aid. These are the elementary steps toward the arousing of dynamic faith. This lesson will teach you how to acquire it.

It is no accident that Jesus nearly always demanded (or assumed) faith on the part of those with whom he worked. Faith is our response to the Word of God. The very presence of Jesus evoked faith. When Jesus really dwells in you, you will produce this effect upon people, your mere presence will inspire faith! You won't try to do this; it will happen naturally, spontaneously!

It is an open secret that, even in medical practice, the doctor who has this buoyancy and confidence regarding the outcome of his treatment (regardless of the particular technique employed) does in a subtle manner communicate a similar quality to his patient, other things being equal. Therefore, as "interns" in the clinic of Jesus, it is our business to study his method, to find out his secrets, to immerse ourselves (so to speak) in the literature of his healing work and thus to keep our eyes fixed on him. By so doing we shall absorb more and more of his spirit and his control over conditions.

When I took my course in therapeutic psychology many years ago, I was greatly impressed with the confidence and quiet assurance of Dr. Sidney A. Weltmer, the head of the college where I was studying. He professed to teach us a psychological technique, but it was obvious that he lived close to God and he frankly admitted that he had begun with an intensive study of the philosophy and method of Jesus as recorded in the four gospels. One of his frequent slogans was this: "You can do what I do, when you know what I know; and I can teach you what I know!" He said this quite simply and without conceit. We knew he had had some marvelous cures. He was trying to arouse our faith in ourselves as well as our faith in God. Jesus spoke similar words to his students, when he exclaimed: "(You) will also do the works that I do."

The Faith in Jesus

What was this faith of Jesus? We assume it with some degree of reverence, but we rarely understand it. Please note I say, "the faith of Jesus," not "faith in Jesus!" We are to cultivate this sort of faith which Jesus had and used. How can we get it? Surely by prayer, quiet meditation and by constant, intelligent, unprejudiced study of the works and method and the very life of Jesus. From such prayer and study (combined) we go right on to experiment, as any science student would do in his laboratory. If we persevere in this, we shall not only succeed in our work but we shall discover the laws which govern divine healing.

Archimedes is sometimes called "The Father of Modern Science" though he lived 200 years before Christ. He insisted that all progress in science depended upon three steps: observation, experiment and calculation. This is still regarded as a scientific attitude. Let us apply it in our study of healing faith.

We observe the works of Jesus as given in the gospel recordings. This is more than a casual glance. We are like medical students in the operating theater of a great hospital, gazing with eager attention to see how the expert surgeon works. Nothing escapes our eager gaze. Nothing is too small for consideration. Having thus observed carefully and frequently we proceed to experiment. Jesus insists upon his "interns" doing this work themselves. He literally "sends them out" two-by-two with definite instructions and assignments. Thus, they are finally able to draw their own conclusions, to make scientific deductions or inferences, the law becomes clear in its working. They can now calculate; they can use the law to bring about certain desired results – they can even discover why certain methods failed to bring results. Describing this faith of Jesus, someone cleverly remarked: "It is not an attitude to be attained; it is an attitude to be maintained!"

This faith of Jesus is not an intellectual attainment, though "right belief" enters into it. It is the result of a life to be lived day-by-day, week-by-week, year-by-year. It is a culture – something cultivated deliberately. For this culture you must pass through the gymnasium of discipleship; this means discipline (the process of becoming a disciple). The Sermon on the Mount (Matthew, chapters 5, 6 and 7) will provide fine training for this course in discipleship. Dr. Fritz Kunkel (in his book, ***Creation Continues***) says that you find no miracles in the Gospel of Matthew until you reach chapter 8. He continues to point out that you must pass through the discipline of chapters 5, 6 and 7 before you can understand the miracles in chapter 8! How much less can you expect to perform such miracles unless you have had training and practice in the principles of Jesus? In the Epistle to the Hebrews, Jesus is described as "the author and finisher [perfecter] of our faith." To contemplate his life, to spend time with him, will inevitably bring about a similar quality in your own life. There is no short cut.

The Faith That Rebels

In a book called ***The Faith that Rebels,*** Dr. D. S. Cairns, for many years Principal of The Church of Scotland College in Aberdeen gives us a wonderful chapter entitled "The Faith of Jesus," which I think is the nearest approach to the sort of faith we are now exploring. There is only room here for a few lines from this chapter. He says the faith of Jesus is woven out of three strands (1) faith in God's power and reality; (2) faith in his love; and (3) faith in his perfect liberty to help men.

> "Power belongs to God."(Psalms 62: 11)
>
> "There is no authority except from God." (Romans 13:1)

This is the first and primitive thing in all religion. Whatever weakens this primitive thing in religion weakens faith. Religion conceives of this power as power over the world. Some prefer to use the term "supreme reality" instead of the "supreme power," because it conveys even more strongly the sense of superiority over the world of appearances. Compared with God the world is a vanishing mist, but it is not a mist beyond his control. Dr. Cairns says:

> It appears to me that Jesus had a unique awareness of the reality and power of God and that he was able to communicate this in a unique degree. With most of us the real plague is 'the seeming unreality of the spiritual life.' The world today is so urgent and so interesting that we can hardly help conceding reality to it in the full sense, and giving only what remains of our energy and thought to God.

This same writer quotes a curious and pathetic passage in one of William James' letters where, in reply to a questionnaire, he says that for himself he has no immediate sense of the divine reality, but that he recognizes that other men, and notably the great mystics, have it, and that he believes their testimony. This is today a very common experience. Even when people have this "open vision," it fluctuates. Great experiences of danger and great scenes in nature suddenly call it forth. Many of us have direct or indirect experiences of this kind in our memories. They do not seem to us hallucinations. Rather do we recognize them as moments of awakening to what is already there. Always there is that sense of power, sovereignty and reality as an essential part of the experience (Cairns, p 219). Faith grows by such experience.

This AWARENESS OF GOD was part of the very substance of the daily life of Jesus. The relationship which, with us, is momentary and transient, was for him unbroken. It is revealed in his words:

> "I do always what is pleasing in his sight." (John 8:29)
>
> "The Father and I are One." (John 10:30)
>
> "...that they may all be one. As you, Father, are in me and I am in you, may they also may be one in us that the world may believe..." (John 17:21)

It comes out even more strikingly in his actions. Look, for instance, at the raising of the daughter of Jairus. Jesus is making his way through the crowd with the father, when the messengers meet them with the fatal words "Your daughter is dead, why trouble the teacher any further?" Anybody else would have taken that word "dead" as final, and turned back. He risked his whole reputation by going on. What was death in comparison with God? That lets us see deep into his spirit. This "going on" is every bit as unique as the wonder which follows. The unique quality of his faith–his spiritual life explains the unique event which followed. How could God be really omnipotent if he could not create what he pleased? God may be limited by creating free human spirits, but cannot be limited by any independent and rival power. This is fundamental to the whole mind of Jesus and is an essential element in his faith.

The Love of God Inspires Faith

Jesus reveals this by his teaching, his "signs," by his whole personality and by his cross. He first teaches man to call God "Father." And surely the miracles are part of this revelation. They show us how we are to think of the divine love and faith, which cares not only for the souls of men, but for their bodies. May I give one further and final quotation from Dr. Cairns:

> They [the miracles] show us that we are to think of Divine Love in the simplest way as delighting in the dispelling of pain, the restoring of sanity, the satisfying of hunger, the preservation of life, the dispelling of premature death, just the things which ordinary human love glories in being able to do. But supreme sacrifice is the most convincing thing of all, when it is freely chosen for love's sake. So by teaching, by living in converse with his fellows, by his "signs" and by his cross, Jesus reveals that the supreme reality is the supreme loving kindness, so that they who receive the revelation know the awakening of faith.
>
> – Cairns, p. 219

God is at Liberty to Help Us

Are you governed and limited by past experience? Most people are so limited. Jesus is the great exception. He is sublimely indifferent to past experience when it obscures God's willingness to help and heal his children. As we develop the real "Christ consciousness," we too are set free from subservience to past measurements of what is possible. As a great philosopher once said: "Principle is not limited by precedent!"

Recall the tone of voice in which your friends speak. Faced by an unusual emergency they exclaim: "Of course with God all things are possible, but..." And you know by that tone of voice that they do not expect to witness any deliverance. Contrast such attitudes with the quiet, positive assurance of our Lord as he faced emergencies, and observe how he breathed the same divine independence into his followers. We dare not measure our duty by our own past experience of what is practicable, but rather learn to estimate the practicable by our independent knowledge of what God lays it on us to undertake.

In his book ***Redemption from This World,*** Professor A. G. Hogg, Madras Christian College (India), says the Christian must never let his visions of the possible and permissible be curbed by the idea that the present life is meant to be a vale of tears. He insists that the miracles of Jesus reveal the truth that in this world pain and disablement and tragedy are intruders hateful to the Heavenly Father and that the New Testament story is an account of the greatest attack in all human history on sin and death. The "supernatural," meaning the divine economy as revealed by Jesus, takes us into larger, higher, wider territory than we have been accustomed to navigate. The faith of Jesus (whether shown in him or in us today) gives God greater freedom to act redemptively than we had ever imagined possible.

The Authority of Faith

Familiarity with the word "*faith*" brings contempt. It is almost necessary to translate it into modern speech to taste its potency and feel its magic touch. The commonest synonym which expresses the idea of faith is *confidence*. You will begin to do these wonderful works when you have developed confidence. It will be confidence of two kinds: (a) confidence in the presence and power of God; and (b) confidence in your ability to realize his presence and to command his power. Let us listen once more to Professor Hogg:

> Vital religion refuses to be put off with evasive vagueness. Where faith is living, it insists on proceeding to particulars, on bringing general convictions to the hard test of concrete present fact. Is it an admitted truth that God grants to people who pray whatever is good for them? Very well! Here is something which I conceive that it would be a real blessing to receive here and now. Either I am mistaken in so thinking, or else God will grant it immediately on my request. This 'either, or' is the mark of living, practical faith... Faith that is living and practical unweariedly presses forward to certainty, certainty about God and certainty about good. So must it have been with the faith of Jesus.

And again:

> His faith would maintain its tension of expectancy, becoming ever more firmly persuaded that an immediate redeeming interposition of God was a thing for which it was right to pray, and which it were an impiety not to expect. (Mark 11:24). The real man of God translates divine omnipresence into a presence of God here and now. He does not solace himself with mere general reflections about God's fatherliness, but expects present succor and support. He is not content with knowing that God requires people to do good, but seeks guidance as to the particular good endeavor which it is God's will that he himself should undertake. Now Jesus was supremely the man of God. There was never an item of man's complexity that did not mean for him God. He never sacrificed the individual to the general mass, or the unexpected opportunity to the preconceived abstract program. Without losing unity of purpose he lived from moment to moment and from individual to individual. Such was the personality with whose later years the records make us familiar. They portray to

> us a soul which from moment to moment envisaged the attitude of a heavenly Father's heart to the particular sins and miseries and the particular sinners and sufferers it beheld on every side.

The Boldness of Faith

Understanding God's heart and ways enables the believer to ask boldly for needed help. Yet, properly understood, it is a mark of genuine faith and there are numerous Scriptures urging us to do this very thing! The best authority is found in Isaiah 45:11: "Thus says the Lord, the Holy One of Israel and its Maker: Will you question me about my children or command me concerning the work of my hands." This remarkable verse comes from a remarkable chapter. You should read the entire chapter, jotting down special verses which inspire your faith; verse 18 is another good example. Also verse 5. "I am the Lord, and there is no other!" Surely that is good doctrine, especially when you think (for the moment) that the Enemy has you at a disadvantage. Best of all is verse 22: "Turn to me, and be saved… for I am God, and there is no other." (v. 18, repeated in v. 22). "I declare what is right." (V. 19).

Here is where Emma Curtis Hopkins gets her famous "High Watch" teaching in which leaders of the healing movement have found themselves for more than sixty years. Here is one of her affirmations based upon this chapter:

The High Watch

> Our initial and compelling faculty is our inner vision.
>
> Vision often Godward and live anew.
>
> So shall the body be like "a tree planted by rivers of water, whose leaf fadeth not."
>
> Vision often Godward so that affairs also may go well.
>
> Gaze often toward our Father, and all thoughts shall be like morning music.
>
> Lift up an inward looking now and then to a country whose ether winds ever raying forth their healing aura, are fleet remedials for all the world's unhappiness.
>
> Emma Curtis Hopkins

Here is another one:

Prayer Of Recognition

> First look to the divine one standing solitary and glorious in the midst of the people of the New Age, saying boldly:
>
> I see you transcending all human conditions, unweighted by matter, unshadowed by fear; free, flawless, triumphant.

> I look now to the Son of God, the Angel of God's Presence, the cure and peace and strength of all mankind.
>
> I look to Everlasting Life, shedding forth the radiance of the everlasting kingdom. All are gathered into life ever renewing, into health ever restoring, into wisdom ever brightening and rejoicing – gathered and upborne in beauty and love and might by Thee, O Free Spirit, victorious Christ Jesus facing me, with face shining as the sun and raiment white as the light, transfiguring the whole earth with living triumph!
>
> Emma Curtis Hopkins

The Meek Shall Inherit

You would naturally think of faith as linked with boldness, and it is, in a certain sense. Thus in Acts, chapters 3-4, we find the apostles who healed the lame man at the Gate Beautiful (see Acts, chapter 3) were charged by the authorities with creating a disturbance (as recorded in the early part of chapter 4). The healing itself was a tremendous act of faith, but the reaction of the bystanders was the tremendous boldness of these men. "When they saw the boldness of Peter and John… they were amazed" (Acts 4:13). It is, therefore, somewhat a paradox when we affirm that the chief prerequisite of healing faith, or any active faith, is meekness. Faith is closely linked with meekness. Meekness has been defined as "gentle receptivity." Different teachers give different emphases in the culture of meekness. In his book ***The Code of Christ,*** Gerald Heard says that the meek are the "trained," and he makes out a fine case for this interpretation. In a more recent book on the Beatitudes (***The Divine Constitution*** by Charles Z. Smith), the author tells us meekness is synonymous with humility, that it is nonresistance. He says a meek man rises above trouble; he is not annoyed, vexed, irritated, disturbed or disappointed. "His heart is perpetually quiet." He further emphasizes that "a truly meek man refuses to strive with false conditions. He is courageous, persistent, steadfast and enduring in his faith in God." Perhaps we can see why Jesus declared that the meek shall inherit the earth!

Moses is considered to be the classic example of the meek man, yet he became the great lawgiver with almost unqualified authority. For more than half a lifetime he announces God's plan for his people in such phrases as "according to the word of the Lord."

Then toward the end of his career we suddenly find (as we study his story) a verse which affirms "and God did as Moses requested!" It is those who have learned to align their thinking and living with the laws of God who are later vested with divine authority in the affairs of humanity.

On this important aspect of faith I would like to quote again from Emma Curtis Hopkins:

> Long before the time of Elijah and Elisha it had been taught in mystic language that we rise up with that authority before which we have been meek. Was not Isaiah meek before the Lord of Hosts till the Lord of Hosts told him to command the Lord of Hosts as an obedient Servitor? Was not Jeremiah meek before the ruler in the heavens and the earth till the ruler in the heavens and the earth told him to show himself ruler over the nations and over the kingdoms? Did not Jesus say, 'Have the rulership of God himself,' when he told his disciples to 'have the faith of God'? (Mark 11:22). For is not faith rulership? Is not faith kingship or confidence to command? (The word 'king' means etymo-logically the man who can.) Is not kingship always associated with confidence to command? 'If you have faith the size of a mustard seed you will say to this mountain, "Move from here

> to there"; and it shall move; and nothing shall be impossible for you.' (Mark 11:22–24)[5]

So we do not identify God as a disciplinarian or one who inflicts hardships or deprivation, instead God is loving presence waiting for us to ask boldly according to his will. Jesus prayed, "Father, glorify me." David asked, "Prosper me." Job asked, "Answer me." Joshua spoke to the Lord and then commanded the sun and moon to stand still; and they did. Hebrews 4:16 says, "Let us therefore approach the throne of grace with boldness, so that we may receive mercy and find grace to help in time of need." Moffatt translates it this way, "Let us approach the throne of grace with confidence."

How to Apply All This

1. Read this chapter over several times.
2. Underscore the lines that stand out for you; or copy them in your notebook.
3. Catch the basic lesson hidden in this chapter. "Inwardly digest" it; assimilate it. "The words that I have spoken to you are spirit and life!" (John 6:63).
4. Let your prayer of faith produce an act of faith!

---

[5] Ibid.

Enter into transactions with God. If his word is true it will stand the test. Learn to say, with Isaiah: "My word… shall not return to me empty, but it shall accomplish that which I purpose, and succeed in the thing for which I sent it." (Isaiah 55:11).

5. Look up the Bible references in your own Bible. Consult with one or more of the modern translations.
6. Catch the timeless element in the Bible. These healing stories are not mere fragments of history. In each story there is the "local situation," the temporary element, the "local color;" but there is also the eternal element. Learn to recapture the story in terms of the living present. You have not adequately studied any of these stories until you discern the divine principle at work there. That divine principle never changes; it belongs as much to you (if you claim it by faith) as to those who were the original beneficiaries of Christ's power.
7. Think of yourself as a potential healer – a "disciple" of the great physician, an intern in his world clinic! You are now fully determined to master the whole of his teaching as you grow more responsive to the urges of his spirit. He has promised to guide you into all truth! (John 16:13)

> As we put out powers that seem to be our own, still even in and by the act of putting them out, we reveal them to be not our own; we discover that we are always

drawing on unseen resources. We are children of God: that is the root law of our entire self.

And faith is the active instinct of the inner sense of being a child of God: it is the point at which that essential relationship emerges into con-sciousness, it is the disclosure to the self of its own vital secret; it is the thrill of our inherent childhood.

From Lux Mundi. These lines were written by the Rev. H. Scott Holland, Canon of St. Paul's, London.

Parallel Reading

Almost any good book on spiritual healing contains useful instruction on faith and how it is developed. The following are merely a few good examples of this:

The Will of God by Leslie D. Weatherhead. The difference between God's will and our own… separates confusion and pain from serenity and change.

Salvation and Wholeness by John P. Baker. A study in the biblical perspectives of healing.

Christ Healing by E. Howard Cobb. A fair-minded, convincing and courageous book, based on scripture and sound reasoning.

Healing by Francis MacNutt, O.P. A comprehensive book on healing by the foremost authority on the healing ministry.

The Power to Heal by Francis MacNutt, O.P. A moving and powerful witness to the healing action of the Spirit.

Will thou Be Made Whole? by Rufus J. Womble, D.D. Jesus promised healing of the whole person: body, mind and soul. Here to inspire you are actual accounts of this promise working today.

Healing Is for Real by Malcolm H. Miner. Malcolm Miner knows the healing and reconciling power of God.

Many resources on healing ministry may be obtained from The International Order of St. Luke, PO Box 780909, San Antonio, TX 78278-0909

Questions

1. How do we maintain the faith of Jesus?
2. Jesus said several times, "Your faith has made you whole." What was their faith in, according to Banks?
3. On page 152-154, seven suggestions are given for applying our faith. Share what you have done as an "act of faith" in the last week or two or three?

IX

THE WORD OF HEALING

"ONLY SPEAK THE WORD and my servant will be healed!"

– Matthew 8:8

"IT IS OUT OF THE ABUNDANCE of the heart that the mouth speaks!"

– Luke 6:45

"MAN'S MOUTH utters what his heart is full of" is Moffatt's translation of this verse (Luke 6:45). The heart of Jesus is full of love and compassion, and out of this abundance he speaks the word which ensures the cure of the Centurion's servant. HIS WORD is not limited to the days of his earthly ministry. Today there are millions of lips through which he speaks this word of love and healing. All we need is a little quiet attention – the hearing ear and the understanding heart, and his deathless words radiate to our point of greatest need and the work is done. It is as simple as our own radio set. We tune in to the right station; we adjust our mechanism of reception and over the waves of invisible ether comes the truth we crave – the truth which will bring release and healing.

Recordings Available

We depend greatly upon recordings of all kinds today; tape recordings, transcribed recordings from original radio and TV programs, bring to our living room the words or the music we want to hear. As modern science brings to perfection these modes of reproducing the words or the melody we keenly desire to hear, let us not discount the ageless recordings made for us in the gospel records in print, which anyone may read. We preachers of the gospel today are accused of too much quotation, too many texts, too many flowery phrases. But "a word fitly spoken, how good it is!"

Do you realize how powerful are the recorded *WORDS* of Jesus which accompany his recorded acts of healing? Your imagination must create a TV set in your own consciousness if you would recapture the power and winsomeness of these mighty acts. The picture alone is not enough. The "silent movie" is a thing of the past. The drama must be completed. Words and action must synchronize. Give your imagination a little exercise. See if you can quickly furnish the dramatic setting for these verses:

> "He cast out the spirits with a word!"
>
> – Matthew 8:16

> "What kind of utterance is this! For with authority and power he commands the unclean spirits, and out they come."
>
> – Luke 4:36

> "Go, your son will live! And the man believed the word that Jesus spoke to him, and started on his way."
>
> – John 4:50

You May Ask Questions of Jesus

"Familiarity breeds contempt" (to quote an old proverb) and we have heard the healing stories about Jesus so often that we think we know all about them. Only the keen seeker will hear Jesus speak today. And you can exercise your soul in this quest by deliberately "hearing him speak." First, in these gospel recordings, ask questions about what you read. Take nothing for granted. Use your intelligence as you watch Jesus at work. Ask such questions as these: "Why did Jesus say that?" "What did he mean by these words?" "What did the sick man understand by this action?" "What is the principle back of this miracle (or that one)?" Let us try this out, using the ninth chapter of the Gospel of Matthew and taking verses eighteen to thirty-eight. Here are four miracles very briefly narrated.

1. The Raising of Jairus' Daughter

Matthew 9:18-26

What is the dominant idea in the mind of Jesus as he performs this remarkable work? Radical, sweeping, paradoxical as it may seem, the dominant idea which emerges from Christ's attitude is the non-reality of death! The leader said, "My daughter has just died; but come and lay your hand on her and she will live." (v. 18). Here is honesty regarding the facts. Here is faith regarding the outcome. When Jesus had eliminated the hysterical and noisy crowd of mourners, he simply declared: "Go away, for the girl is not dead, but sleeping!" (v. 24). (Moffatt gives it: "Begone; the girl is not dead but asleep!")[1] Holding to this great principle of the non-reality of death, Jesus does his work. "But when the crowd had been put outside, he went in and took her by the hand, and the girl got up." (v. 25).

If you say this was simply a case of suspended animation, I reply that Jesus repeated similar words on each of the three occasions in which he raised the dead as recorded in the gospels. Even in the case of Lazarus, who had been dead four days before Jesus reached him, he said, "Our friend Lazarus has fallen asleep; but I am going there to awaken him." Only when he found his disciples misunderstanding his words did he substitute

---

[1] Moffatt, op. cit.

the word "death" (see John 11: 11-15). To the early Christians "death" was always regarded as "sleep."

2. The Woman with the Hemorrhage

Matthew 9:20-22

The principle back of this healing is the *power of faith*. You don't have to guess at it. The Word of Jesus states it explicitly: "Take heart, daughter; your faith has made you well!" (v.22). As the woman's faith responded to the Word of Jesus, so your faith can respond to the Word of Jesus, with similar or identical results. Perhaps you ask: How did this woman express such a faith as this? The answer is simple: She talked to herself about Jesus. This is the next best thing to talking with Jesus. She said within herself: "If I only touch his cloak, I will be made well!" That is genuine faith expressed in simple words. Her conscious mind was talking to her subconscious mind. She (conscious) said to herself (subconscious) "If I only touch..." And when your conscious mind agrees with your subconscious mind, things begin to happen; you are then at one with yourself. You are like the prodigal son in the far country longing to get back home: "And when he came to himself he said..." As we come near to Jesus we come near to our true selves – that is the magical secret that brings healing. No doubt the faith of Jesus inspired and evoked the woman's faith. The faith of Jesus is shown in the "virtue" that flowed from him, even radiating through his garment. The faith of the woman is shown in her determination to make contact with him: "If I only touch..." It is also shown in her belief that such a contact would bring instantaneous healing. When these two elements meet, healing always results. I often see it at a mission of healing, or at any local healing service. The minister lifts up his hand (as though to invoke the waiting blessing); he then lays his hands on the seeker kneeling at the altar. The faith of the seeker responds and joins with the faith of the minister and others who are praying. The same act of the laying on of hands simultaneously invokes God's healing power and evokes the latent faith of the seeker. That is why it seems to form the most direct and dynamic spiritual treatment.

3. Two Blind Men Healed

Matthew 9:27-31

The principle here is that personal faith in our Lord leads to an attitude of eager expectancy. This is another name for faith. It always brings healing. The clue to this miracle is found in the words of Jesus to these blind men: "Do you believe that I am able to do this?" (Matthew 9:28). And they said unto him: 'Yes, Lord.'" Then Jesus said and did something to arouse their faith. "Then he touched their eyes, saying, 'According to your faith be it to you!'" (v. 29). What a heavy responsibility lies upon the clergy and others who minister directly to the sick for being so overloaded with caution and fear of failure that they often fail dismally to draw out the latent faith of the patient. The cure of unbelief on the part of the clergy and other workers is often a harder miracle than the cure of disease in the patient.

4. The Mute Demon Cast Out

Matthew 9:32-35

We can *describe* the working principle at work here; we cannot *define* it. It is simply the power that resides in the word of Jesus. His word is the breathing forth of a specific energy, we might say a force, charged with incredible power, a force which simply annihilates the spell of evil resident in the patient. May we remind our readers, once again, of the significance of this word *"spell."* It is associated with credulity and superstition; yet, it is a useful word full of meaning. It implies the power of one mind over another mind (or other minds). It is more often used in a sinister sense though it need not imply any evil influence. Magicians and charlatans in medieval Europe, and even today in some countries, placed a "spell" on certain people. These spells had a sort of hypnotic efficacy. Exorcists, from time immemorial, have claimed the power to break these spells and to deliver those who were thus obsessed. In the early Church many of the candidates for the priesthood were first ordained as "exorcists." In many cases this was merely the Church's way of recognizing a "gift" already possessed by the candidate. They exorcised "in the name of Jesus." They invoked his greater power to subdue the evil (but lesser) power of the obsessing influence. All this was a legitimate and integral part of the gospel ministry, for the word "gospel" means, literally, "God's spell." How tremendously our present-day world needs this potent exorcism of "God's spell" to overcome the various obsessions, inhibitions, dementias and fixations of the world, the flesh and the devil! As you read these lines, ponder the possibility that you may latently possess this power of exorcism. "Be not overcome of evil, but overcome evil with good!" Sometimes this calls for direct, radical, uncompromising attack in the name of Jesus.

This particular lesson is not primarily on exorcism, but we insist that it be regarded as an intrinsic part of the healing ministry of Jesus, which we are commissioned to carry on in our own day and in our own environment. Jesus drew no hard and fast line between ordinary "healing" and the use of exorcism. In commissioning his followers especially the twelve and the seventy he specifically included the casting out of demons, along with the healing of the sick and the proclaiming of the evangel, that is preaching. What God has joined together, let no one separate.

In my own ministry in public and in private, I have never emphasized exorcism; but I have used it when challenged by the forces of the enemy and was surprised to see how quickly it worked, even with the minimum of preparation on the part of the patient. Needless to say, the guided disciple will learn quickly to differentiate between a case of demonization (as such) and the case of simple or complex mental disorder, which is in quite another category.

The tracing of the principles and implications in these few verses in regard to four healing works of Jesus can be indefinitely extended. These cases are recorded consecutively. Doubtless they were observed by the original chronicler, who first wrote this gospel, or the data on which it is based. These cases are not very different from the types we might meet within any modern mission of healing, or healing camp, or other place where needy men and women come for Christ's Word and touch. Study all you want to about spiritual diagnosis, about pastoral psychology and the best works of modern spiritual therapy; the simple basic fact remains that these inspired records of the healing of Jesus furnish us with sound and reliable data for an effective ministry to the suffering, whether in mind or body.

These records have never been studied with the depth and skill, with the incisive vision and penetration of mind which they deserve. When we study them, we shall begin to practice their teaching.

A true philosophy of Christian healing will be constructed out of the sum total of principles of truth which we see exemplified in all the recorded miracles of Jesus.

The Pragmatic Test

When such careful, thoughtful, prayerful and painstaking study is undertaken – whether by individuals or groups – we shall begin to find corroboration of the Gospel message in our own up-to-the-minute experience. Personal interviews, prayer clinics, healing camps, local prayer groups, as well as the larger efforts contemplated by a mission of healing or an organized healing center, will furnish abundant evidence that the method of Jesus still "works" and that the master method is "the Master's method!"

One of the astounding things which we see emerging from the gospel narratives is that Jesus claims no monopoly in this work. The ministry of healing which he exercises is a ministry he wants to share with his followers. We are so familiar with his recorded utterances that we often lose their meaning. Thus, for example, "The one who believes in me will also do the works that I, and, in fact will do greater works than these, because I go to the Father." (John 14:12). Filled with and guided by his Spirit, which he promised definitely, these words of Jesus should be fulfilled in the life of each follower today. Failure to produce these "greater works" is not so much due to lack of training, in the technical sense, as to lack of sheer belief in the authority of Christ's words for us and lack of faith in attempting the work he commands. The mischievous doctrine that these miracles were guaranteed to the disciples of the first century as credentials for Jesus and then withdrawn as no longer necessary is ridiculous.

The quality of discipleship required in the work of healing is peculiar. It involves perennial discipline; it requires a life lived in close contact with God through his son Jesus Christ. It calls for a life constantly and consciously replenished by the unfailing power of the Holy Spirit. This becomes possible by means of frequent times of quiet prayer, as well as seasons of deep fellowship with those who are treading the same path.

Granted these principles and this discipline, there is no reason why any priest or pastor or other dedicated leader should fail in the exercise of healing under right conditions. Indeed, I feel God wills for many laymen and laywomen to exercise this gift. It is part of the proclamation of the new order in the Church, the truly ecumenical Church whereby we are rising above the shackles of tradition and the mediocre attainments of organized Christianity to meet the challenge of our Lord Jesus Christ for this present age.

Jesus commands his followers to heal the sick! How far are you obeying his commands?

Summary

1. The Word, uttered through the mouth, reveals the heart.
2. The Word is multiplied and broadcast through records whether in the printed page, or by letter, or electrically by radio or TV.
3. The Christian gospels furnish us with reliable records. We may actually know "the mind of Christ" for today's task.
4. Prayer gives us contemporary light on these records. We may actually know "the mind of Christ" for today's task.
5. Through inspired imagination the gospels may become for us contemporary documents, as though we saw them acted out today.
6. The healing of the sick, the casting out of demons, and the actual raising of the (so-called) dead are all part of Christ's ministry of healing. We should relate them as such.
7. We must learn the underlying principle in each miracle. These are all emphasized in this lesson. For the raising of the dead, the principle is "the non-reality of death,"

which may be logically inferred from the words of Jesus in each record of a raising given in the gospels.

The principle in the case of the woman with a hemorrhage is the power of faith in which we see the attitude of eager expectancy and the ability of the conscious mind to talk to the subconscious: "She said to herself...." We also discern here the value of acting out objectively the faith we hold subjectively.

The same principle of eager expectancy as the basis of faith is shown in the cure of the two blind men. Belief is subjective (inward); faith is both subjective and objective. We must see the relevance of the question asked by Jesus: "Do you believe that I am able to do this?" When this question is answered in the affirmative (and perhaps only then) Jesus can exclaim:

> "According to your faith, let it be to you ."
> – Matthew 9:29

The principle back of the case of exorcism is simply that good, if present in sufficient potency can always overcome evil! The command to "cast out demons" might be paraphrased by the Apostle Paul's exhortation: "Do not be overcome by evil, but overcome evil with good.

8. Close examination of this lesson shows why the Church in its larger and organized sense is so inadequate in healing today. It lacks authority, courage, faith and a basic understanding of the simple technique which Jesus used and enjoined.

9. The pragmatic test is found in the testing of faith by works.
10. The quality of discipleship depends on utter loyalty to the example as well as the actual words of Jesus. Lack of discipline produces a low grade of discipleship. A high standard of discipline is reached through a high standard of love and prayer, secretly in the heart, and outwardly in fellowship with other disciples.

Questions

1. Look up the dramatic settings for Matt. 8:16, Luke 4:36, John 4:50. Describe.
2. Read Matt. 9:18-38. List four conditions that were healed.

   a.

   b.

   c.

   d.

   In which ones is faith mentioned or expressed in some way and by whom?
3. What were Jesus' conclusions in verses 9:36-38?
4. What were the conclusions of the Pharisees?
5. What do the healings of Jesus mean for your ministry?

X

HOW TO RECEIVE HEALING

"What can this Gospel of Jesus be?
What Life and Immortality,
What was it that he brought to Light
That Plato and Cicero did not write?

It was when Jesus said to me
'Thy sins are all forgiven thee,'
Loud Pilate howl'd, loud Caiphas yelled
When they the Gospel Light beheld.
It was when Jesus said to me
'Thy sins are all forgiven thee.'
The Christian trumpets loud proclaim
Through all the world in Jesus' Name
Mutual forgiveness of each vice
And oped the gates of Paradise."

– William Blake (***The Everlasting Gospel***, ca. 1818)

WE ACCEPT HEALING in principle, but reject it in practice. We authorize it in the Prayer Book, read books (and write books) about it, attend healing services, organize healing prayer groups. But having done all these things it often happens we fail to receive this healing for ourselves. There is really no mystery about this. There are excellent reasons to explain both our success and our failure. There are no accidents. There are laws which we recognize and obey, or disobey (even unconsciously) and these require study, patience and perseverance. God is no respecter of person; but God is a respecter of conditions, and when those conditions are satisfied the results follow. This chapter is to help you to understand these conditions which bring healing. It is also to help you to create within yourself these conditions.

1. First Comes Forgiveness

This has become a platitude among teachers and evangelists of Christian healing. Therefore, I have brought it to your notice in the form of a poem by William Blake written 135 years ago. The very quaintness of his language may help you to see this fact of forgiveness (human and divine) as central to all redemptive activity, whether it relates to healing for the body or salvation for the soul.

There is a sequence in healing which must never be overlooked – it follows a spiritual law which may be found working all through religious history. This law is reflected in both the Old and New Testament writings. Its simplest expression is in Psalm 103: "Bless the Lord, O my soul... who forgives all your iniquity; who heals all your diseases and who redeems your life from the pit (destruction)." First forgiveness, then healing and finally complete wholeness, i.e. salvation!

Forgiveness brings healing because it is the absolution of the soul. The body constantly records and reflects the dominant condition of the soul. You can't influence one without influencing the other. As Edmund Spenser wrote more than four centuries ago,

> For of the soul the body form doth take,
> For soul is form and doth the body make.
>
> "Ode to Beauty"

We shall deal elsewhere with this cardinal topic of forgiveness, but let it stand here in the first place in this sequence of how healing comes!

2. Medicine

Medicine is included here as a channel of healing, not a source of healing. Modern medicine by the very phrase limits itself to the physical plane. A medical practitioner is described as a "physician" – i.e. one dealing with the physical aspect of healing. And though the word is used today in a larger connotation (e.g. psychiatric medicine; psychosomatic medicine; etc., etc.), still it is limited in many minds to the treatment of the body. While this fact is accepted, it need not discourage us from seeing in modern medicine a means or channel through which many prayers are answered, a channel used by God as taught in Holy Scripture. In the Book of Common Prayer you will find the passage appointed for the First Lesson on St. Luke's Day is taken from the Book of Sirach in the Apocrypha, Chapter 38, verses 1-14.

> Honor physicians for their services, for the Lord created them; for their gift of healing comes from the Most High... The Lord created medicines out of the earth, and the sensible will not despise them... And he gave skill to human beings that he might be glorified in his marvelous works. By them the physician heals and takes away pain ... My child, when you are ill, do not delay, but pray to the Lord, and he will heal you.

Read further in this chapter and you will find it recognizes disease for what it really is:

> He who sins against his Maker, will be defiant toward the physician.

And again:

> Give up your faults and direct your hands rightly, and cleanse your heart from all sin... Then give the physician his place, for the Lord created him.

In my extensive collection of books on spiritual therapy, I am interested to note that many of them are written by qualified physicians.[1]

I do not claim that medical science is in itself spiritual; but when the physician himself (or herself) becomes spiritual, this special skill and training can become a tremendous power for direct spiritual healing.

3. Spiritual Therapy Treats the Patient

In using any of the methods outlined in this book, please remember that we are not treating disease; we are treating the patient! This may seem obvious to some; but it has to be consciously learned by others. It is always the patients themselves who need healing. Dr. Alexis Carrel felt this so powerfully that it became his main thesis in the book ***Man, The Unknown***. The practice of healing seeks ultimately that essential wholeness of the entire being of the patient. The word *"whole"* in the original is practically identical with its synonyms; soundness, salvation and sanctification, though each of these words by long usage has acquired a distinct and peculiar meaning. It is worthwhile to refer the reader to a verse in the Bible as evidence of this identity. That verse is Luke 1:77:

[1] John Rathbone Oliver of Baltimore, Claude O'Flaherty of Scotland, Rebecca Beard of St. Louis, and dozens of others.

"To give knowledge of salvation to his people by the forgiveness of their sins."

That phrase "knowledge of salvation" in the Latin Vulgate reads: "*scientia salutis*" which might quite properly be translated "*the science of health*" and is so translated in the Wycliffe version of the Bible. Imagine the consternation of the people if a modern Protestant minister announced his text some fine Sunday morning: "You will go before the Lord... to give the science of health to his people by the forgiveness of their sins!" (Luke 1:76-77). Yet such announcement might be clearer to the average layman (and bring him or her closer to the original meaning) than if he said "to give the knowledge of salvation," since the fine old word "salvation" is today overlaid with every brand of theological bias, depending upon the background and religious affiliations of the preacher! But the term *science of health* could hardly be used ambiguously. Some people believe that Mary Baker Eddy found the title of her famous book from the Wycliffe translation of this verse! Every Christian – no matter what his church, or background, or religious affiliation – might profitably bear in mind that the *knowledge of salvation* and the *science of health* are interchangeable and equivalent phrases. Perhaps we will become more zealous in acquiring this sort of "knowledge of salvation" when we realize that it includes also the elements of health and healing!

4. Spiritual Healing Restores Right Conditions

The Apostle Peter declares (Acts 10:34), "God is no respecter of persons (KJV)," but he is very much a respecter of conditions! To a large extent we ourselves make those conditions in which he can heal us. Disease develops from wrong conditions; these must be corrected as far as possible. This was the method of Jesus himself. When he found the paralytic helpless and saw intuitively the cause back of the physical malady, Jesus wasted no time with palliatives. He went after the ultimate cause of the trouble and firmly declared: "Son, your sins are forgiven!" (Mark 2:5). When the critics, religious men, found fault with this technique, Jesus vindicated himself in words that reflected sound psychology mixed with sound religion:

> "Why do you raise such questions in your hearts? Which is it easier to say to the paralytic, 'Your sins are forgiven'; or to say, 'Stand up and take your mat and walk'? But so that you may know that the Son of Man has authority on earth to forgive sins," he said to the paralytic, "I say to you, stand up and take your

> mat and go to your home." And he stood up, and immediately took the mat and went out before all of them, so that they were all amazed...
>
> – Mark 2:8-11

Jesus was no magician. He claimed his disciples could do anything he could do, because he had given them his spirit. He cast out demons by the finger of God, but he told his disciples to do the same thing. When he saw the deaf mute inhibited by the crowds, he took him aside and treated him privately to avoid embarrassment. His love was no pleasant altruism or mere attitude of benevolence, but an active healing agent which flowed forth from his aura wherever he went. Even in our own time we have had examples of this same outgoing virtue which can heal medically incurable patients in some cases.

Father Fitzgerald of The Community of the Resurrection, an Anglican Order in Britain, could cure homicidal maniacs because (a) he loved them; and (b) he was not afraid of them. I have personally listened to his stories, always told very humbly, almost reluctantly, but very convincingly. What are spiritually-minded people today doing for the cure of the insane? Do we know even how to pray intelligently for those who suffer from mental and emotional disorders?

5. Techniques May Be Used

Many devout people are suspicious of "techniques." They would say these belong exclusively to the physician or psychiatrist. But the long history of the Church reveals the successful use of many and varied techniques for the healing of the sick. For detailed examples see the section on "The Visitation of the Sick" by Dr. Charles Harris in the book ***Liturgy and Worship***.[1] What are some of these techniques?

(a) The prayer of faith, which should accompany any technique.

(b) The laying-on of hands, perhaps the most popular, the most simple and the most effective of all techniques, ancient or modern. See Mark 16:18.

(c) The anointing with oil, sometimes called "Holy Unction," which the Church has recognized as a sacrament for centuries.

(d) The ministry of absolution, especially the declaration of the forgiveness of sins, usually preceded by some form of confession. Protestant churches need to study this carefully.

(e) Analysis, or some other kind of psychological treatment, done with a spiritual motive, for the relieving of moral and emotional complexes which burden the patient. Many clergy have qualified

---

[1] Clarke and Harris, published by S.P.C.K., London and Macmillan, New York.

themselves by special training for this sort of work; but it is usually done by practitioners other than clergy. The treatment of the woman at the well of Sychar (described in John 4) is actually a condensed account of a simple analysis done by Jesus. Modified forms of this method are now to be found in all up-to-date textbooks of pastoral psychology, and this technique is successfully used by hundreds of good pastors and priests who have acquainted themselves with the moral and emotional problems of their parishioners. Dean F. S. M. Bennett of Chester, England, was one of the first to use this technique systematically and he wrote a little book about it entitled *Psycho-synthesis*. More modern treatises would include *Psychiatry and Mental Health*[2] and *Pastoral Psychiatry*[3].

6. Spiritual Healing is a Spiritual Gift ("Charisma")

This ministry, as used historically, implies a spiritual "gift" or *charisma*. This term is actually employed in the original Greek text – see 1 Cor. 12:4 and elsewhere in that chapter. There are many of these gifts of grace, "*charismata,*" healing is but one of them. Many clergy and laity have these gifts latently but have never discovered them or learned to use them. They are not

[2] by John Rathbone Oliver (priest and physician).
[3] by John Sutherland Bonnell of New York

private and personal possessions, they belong to the whole Church, but they become available through individuals thus endowed. Read the whole 12th chapter of 1 Corinthians for Apostle Paul's teaching on all this. The Apostle Paul used this gift himself and described it as a gift of the Spirit. It must not be treated as something proprietary by those through whom it functions. Many of the early Church fathers had this healing gift and refer to it in their writings.[4]

7. Spiritual Therapy Has a Goal

The goal of divine healing is nothing less than the healing of the entire human family – bodily, mentally, spiritually, morally, politically, emotionally and every other way. The individual is to be healed not just for himself, but that he may become a channel for the healing of the world! No one of us is entirely unrelated to this task of healing. I once heard a speaker in Oxford put it thus: "This is a very sick world. Are you part of the disease? or are you part of the cure?" The goal or objective of divine healing is the demonstrating in human experience of the kingdom of God. But this phrase has become so commonplace by over-use that we have to put it into different words. Moffatt

---

[4] see Dr. Evelyn Frost's remarkable book ***Christian Healing*** for examples. Also refer to Father John of Cronstadt, James Moore Hickson of London, John Maillard of Milton Abbey, Agnes Sanford of Massachusetts, and many others.

translates it "The Reign of God." Dr. F. J. Hort, the great English Bible scholar, says the kingdom of God is "that world of invisible laws by which God is ruling and blessing his creatures." Dr. Sanday acquiesces in this definition. Dr. A. B. Bruce, great Scottish theologian, declared it was "The reign of divine love exercised by God in his grace over human hearts believing in his love." We do not need any further definition– what we need is demonstration! In Matthew alone the expressions "kingdom of heaven" and "kingdom of God" occur forty-five times; and generally the theme seems never to have been absent for a single hour from the thoughts of Jesus during his earthly ministry. The greatest healing prayer in the world is "Your kingdom come... your will be done on earth, as it is done in heaven." Never forget Jesus said, "Your will be done" – not your will be suffered!" The former implies a positive attitude where you identify yourself with the health-giving purposes of God – his wholeness and his holiness. The latter is passive; it should be used only in a very limited category. This healing will of God is one aspect of the divine work of redemption. Divine healing is a contagion of life; it spreads through those who receive it. It aims at complete integration – perfect wholeness. It produces the fruits of sanctification in the best and highest sense of that word.

8. Should We Expect Results?

Most certainly we should expect results. This attitude of "expectancy" is an essential part of your reception. Indeed it was at a healing clinic in Nancy, France that the definition was first coined: "Faith is the attitude of eager expectancy." The gospels evoke this attitude of eager expectancy – the mere reading of the gospels will do this. The preaching of the gospel will do this, if the preacher himself is animated by this attitude. Reading parts of the gospels in a unified prayer group – with pauses for silence, praise and witness – will powerfully evoke this attitude of eager expectancy. There is a residue of power – a mysterious and cumulative residue of power – in the gospels that baffles analysis but encourages prayer activity. After more than thirty years of healing mission work I can testify that nothing in my experience equals the sheer spiritual stimulation of a concentrated study of the gospel miracles, accompanied by frequent intervals for prayer and contemplation. Faith comes from what is heard, and what is heard comes through the Word of Christ (Romans 10:17). What word is this? The same chapter gives the answer: "The Word is near you, on your lips and in your heart, that is the word of faith that we proclaim." (Romans 10:8). We should expect results because Jesus told us to expect them. We find this assurance at the end of the Gospel of

Mark: "These signs will accompany those who believe... They shall lay their hands on the sick, and they shall recover." (Mark 16:17-18). If those words are an addition, or an interpolation, to the original narrative, the facts of Christian history nevertheless fully bear out their truth. It is the pragmatic test which authenticates absolute faith in God. Faith in God and love for people are the only two indispensable prerequisites for divine healing. The results of this ministry are to be seen not only in bodily and mental healing, but in a quickening of all spiritual activities. Let me quote from a little book by Bishop Conkling of Chicago written while he was a parish priest in Philadelphia: "It is not surprising that the practice of spiritual healing in a parish should bring new converts to faith for baptism and confirmation, increase the number of penitents and communions, and this has been found to be true. More than that it has brought many wandering sheep home to the fold, and who can blame them for having wandered, if, to use Milton's phrase:

"The hungry sheep look up and are not fed..."

The bishop continues: "These are all worth-while and remarkable results, but we still make answer to the question: Do you actually heal people? It is splendid to make the clergy pray better and be better pastors – and that the people should like-wise pray better, and the parish sacramental life can be deepened and enriched, but is this all that you can achieve by what you call spiritual healing? The answer is, of course, that physical healing is frequently manifested through such spiritual ministrations. There are what we call 'failures,' but there are many notable successes, and these are of many types."

I could fill several chapters of this book with examples I have witnessed with my own eyes, but do not feel led to do so here. If you want clinical examples of divine healing, read Elsie Salmon's exciting book ***He Heals Today*** or the pamphlets published by Louise Eggleston, or the two books of Dorothy Kerin, ***The Living Touch*** and ***Fulfilling***, or ***Recovery*** by Starr Daily for results achieved in a Chicago pastorate.

9. Who Can Heal?

There seems to be a widespread idea that only very saintly persons can exercise the ministry of divine healing. This is a misleading notion, yet it contains an element of truth. The more selfless a person becomes, the more effective healing he or she can perform. The more selfish a person is, the less healing he or she can perform. A saint is hardly ever what we call a pious person, but he or she is a person whose ego is in process of being superseded by the higher self (or the Christ Self). The Apostle Paul says we are all called to be saints (1 Cor 1:2). The very word needs renovating! Here is a very modern definition of saints. I quote from Gerald Heard's book ***The Creed of Christ***:

> Who are saints? They are simply men or women who permit God's forgiveness to come into them so fully that not only are their sins cleansed, but also their very selves, their egos, and the root of their self-will. And, again we see the intensity of their power really to forgive is in exact proportion to the degree that they have permitted themselves to be forgiven and so brought back to God.
>
> (work cited, p130)

It would be almost true to say that you can re-write this quotation, substituting the word *"heal"* for the word *"forgive,"* and the words would still hold good. The next paragraph from the same book deepens this impression:

> I forgive to the level that I have been forgiven, and if that level is moderate (because I made reservations in what I declared because I only wanted to lose my vices and not myself), I can forgive only people who have offended moderately, and my forgiveness helps them only moderately. If I try forgiving people who have wronged me or others intensely, I

> find either I can't do it at all or the quality of my forgiveness is so weak that it is either resented (as the maniac became more fierce as the disciples tried to cure him) or more often dismissed with contempt.

We lack power on earth to forgive sins because we are not forgiven to that degree – to that degree that God is our sole end and our egotism is no more!

10. Healing Skills

Use the healing skills you already possess, and they will surely increase and enlarge. The very desire and effort to bring about healing in other people will help you to transcend your own ego and come more closely into union with the divine. Use more generously the agencies mentioned above; encourage and assist those whom you know to be actively engaged in healing ministry; study the subject in all its fascinating aspects. Do this, and the ministry of healing will come back once again into its rightful place in the life of the Church.

11. Your Own Personal Healing

For those who have learned to use the language of mystical devotion I recommend the ***Studies in High Mysticism***, written by Emma Curtis Hopkins sixty years ago. Here is an example,

Begin with yourself, to repent, to return.
Lift up the willing inner sight toward the Supreme One,
Whose soundless edict through the ages is:
'Look unto Me and be ye saved!'
Taste the first manna which the upward watch sprinkles over the unfed brain and heart.
This is a reasonable service. It is mirific obedience.
Vision often Godward and live anew.
So shall the body be like 'a tree planted by rivers of water, whose leaf fadeth not.'
Vision often Godward so that affairs also may go well.
Gaze often towards Our Father, and all thoughts shall be like morning music.
Lift up an inward looking now and then
To a country whose ether winds ever raying forth their healing aura, are fleet remedials for all the world's unhappiness.

– Emma Curtis Hopkins

12. Treatment for Forgiveness

If you need forgiveness and cannot for any reason go to a qualified counselor or priest, try this self-treatment. Go to a quiet place where you will be undisturbed. Get quiet within yourself. Lift up your hands and say (somewhat) as follows:

Surrender to the Most High

HERE IS MY MIND. I spread it out before you!
Forgive its foolishness and ignorance
With your bright wisdom.
HERE IS MY LIFE. I offer it to you.
Forgive its contrariness to you.
HERE IS MY HEART. It is yours only.
Forgive its restlessness and dissatisfaction.
Forgive its discouragements.
Forgive its resentments.
Forgive its loves and its hates - its hopes and its fears.
HERE IS MY BODY. I cast it down before you.
Forgive its imperfection with Thy Perfection.
Forgive me altogether with Thyself. Give for my self Thy Self!

– Emma Curtis Hopkins

This healing formula will prove an unfailing specific if you will use it perseveringly – saying it over several times until you are absolutely at peace – with yourself and with God. Perhaps you do not like repetitions. Then you might remember that Jesus did not say, "Don't be repetitions!" But he did say, "Don't use vain repetitions! " I have found this little formula of great value. It has never been for me a "vain repetition" and I have used it thousands of times.

QUESTIONS

How do we encourage putting the following principles into practice?

1. Forgiveness of others and self.
2. Medicine as a channel of healing.
3. "Knowledge of salvation" and "science of health" as interchangeable and equivalent – how do we help "church" people understand this?
4. Mental illnesses as being given help through the healing power of Jesus?
5. Is spiritual healing a gift and/or a practice to be developed? What have you found?
6. What do you find the most difficult and what do you find the easiest about healing?
7. How can we encourage people to share the healings they have received?
8. What is there about a person that leads you to believe that they could or do act as a healing agent or channel?
9. What do you find helpful in your own personal healing?

XI

HOW YOUR FAITH CAN HEAL OTHERS

> As surely as God is faithful, our word to you has not been "Yes and No." For the Son of God, Jesus Christ, whom we proclaimed among you ... was not "Yes and No"; but in him it is always "Yes." For in him every one of God's promises is a "Yes." For this reason, it is through him that we say the "Amen," to the glory of God.
>
> – 2 Corinthians 1:18-20

THE PROMISES of God are always *yes*, but we have not learned to tune into them so we think they may be *no* for us. Sometimes when we turn to God in prayer, it is with the attitude:

"Eenie, meenie, miney, mo!
It might be 'yes' and it might be 'no'!"

But God's word is always *yes*! You are dealing with the mind of God which is positive and affirmative. It is what is contrary to that mind which is *no*! If you are thinking thoughts that are not in harmony with God, then, of course, you create a *no*.

There is a new book on prayer which will help to make all this clearer to you, It was written by W. Mauleverer, an English clergyman, Rector of a small but historic parish. The book is entitled ***The Prayer of Affirmation.*** Twenty-five years ago this kind of prayer would have been criticized by the clergy as being "too much like Christian Science," but today we know that the affirmation, no matter who uses it, is a Bible technique, and it works. Our task is to learn good affirmations. "The object of our affirmation," as the author of this book says, "is not to bring about a situation which we should like to exist but to see more clearly a situation that has been present all the time." To pray well is to think with God and to allow the pure truth of God to correct all the wrongs in our conscience. We need the clear vision and the clear speaking of the Son of Man. We must immerse ourselves in, saturate ourselves with the sayings of Jesus, live on them day by day, absorb them; then we shall have power to pray and power to heal and power to solve the problems of everyday life. The disciple is disciplined by the words of the Master. Discipline is the process of becoming a disciple and it takes perseverance, persistence, an intelligent indoctrination in the teachings of Jesus. "If you continue in my word, you are truly my disciples." Jesus said, "And you will know the truth and the truth will make you free." (John 8:31-32). The truth of the last part of that statement of our Lord depends upon our acceptance of the truth in the first part. We speak lots of truth but we spoil it by negative ideas. We "think evil" in our hearts, almost without knowing it, and thereby we dilute the power and efficacy of the truth which we really do believe. If we could learn to think with God, we'd get well. When we think evil in our hearts, our bodies respond. If you ever want to do successful work in healing or in intercession or in ministering to those who are mentally or physically ill, you must learn to think with Jesus.

Contrast these two ways of prayer. You are afraid of something – a person, a problem, a duty, an obstacle – and you want to pray about it. You might say, "O God, I'm scared to death of so-and-so, but won't you see me through?" That is not the way the psalmist prayed. He said, "The Lord is my light and my salvation." He was not begging. He was not supplicating. He was making a positive statement of what God is, and of what God meant to him. Then, he went on to make a logical deduction from that: "Whom shall I fear? The Lord is the stronghold of my life, of whom shall I be afraid?" (See Psalm 27). The book of Psalms is filled with these powerful prayers of affirmation. Some of the best Psalms in this respect are Ps. 23, Ps. 46,

Ps. 91, Ps. 103, and Ps. 121. Take Psalm 91:1. You can easily make an affirmation of that. It reads, "You who live in the shelter of the Most High, abide in the shadow of the Almighty." You affirm: "I live in the shelter of the Most High; therefore, I abide in the shadow of the Almighty." You sometimes have to change the third person singular of the verb to the first person singular. You can make many wonderful affirmations for yourself or others, based on the Word of God.

The Bible abounds in marvelous promises. But if I were to ask you for Bible promises, I think I could anticipate the ones you would quote. There are sixteen or eighteen that everybody who is a lover of the Bible will quote. But there are hundreds of them in the Bible, and they are all included in the *yes* that affirms all the promises of God. Seek out and learn the ones that fit your need. Let the spirit of wisdom enlarge your understanding. God always speaks positively. What a glorious thing it is to learn the liberty of the spirit of truth, of Jesus.

Don't read the Bible or hear it read as a record that you love to hear played over and over again. Sometimes we love the sound of the words so much that we entirely miss their meaning. Insist on knowing what you are reading in your Bible study. Don't take for granted that you know the meaning of all the words. What you want to know is – what did God say through the men who wrote under his inspiration? And what is God's message in present, direct, contemporary inspiration.

Use words in their proper sense, you will be rewarded. Read and study the modern translations as well as the older ones. Learn the promises that have previously been unfamiliar to you, but learn to understand the familiar ones in the new and deeper way.

Now, we are going to consider the individual intercessory prayer, and then we shall pass on to consider the work of prayer groups and some of the problems faced by them.

Praying For Others

An intercessor is one who prays for others. Intercession is really an advanced form of prayer, and it is not an easy thing to do. It is greatly needed and every disciple of Jesus should become an intercessor – but do not take it too lightly. Someone says, "Will you pray for Harry? He's having a very bad time!" Or a woman friend of yours, Emily, has had an automobile accident. She is not in danger of losing her life, but she is considerably crippled and needs much hospital care. You are asked to pray for Emily. Or you have a son in the army. He is drinking too much and living a rather wild life. You've heard about it and you are worried about it. His name is Tom.

Now, stop for a moment and ask yourself just what you are going to say to God. Are you going to tell God that Harry is having a bad time? God knows much more about it than you do; you don't have to inform him. How will you actually represent Harry in your prayer to God, being sincere and straightforward in your words, and yet with the object of doing Harry some good. Will you tell God all about Emily's accident? He knows the facts. You do not have to relate them to him. How do you bring the virtues, the resources of God, the love of Christ, the healing power of the Holy Spirit to Emily, the victim of this accident. Or, take your son. Would you go to God and say, "Tom is getting rather wild, a bit out of hand. He is drinking too much and in the wrong kind of company. O God, can you do something about it?" You could pray that way, of course, but it would not be an ideal intercession.

The following technique has helped me immeasurably and it may help you. There are many methods of intercession; this is not the only one. First, get quiet. This might take two or three minutes. Rushing into God's presence is not the ideal way. Say something like this to him: "O God, take these few minutes of my time and accept my desire to help these, your servants." The keynote of prayer is this opening quietness: "Speak, Lord, for your servant is listening."

We reverse the order many times and say, "Listen, Lord, for your servant is speaking." Offer your love, your will, your time (perhaps fifteen minutes or more), your imagination to God on behalf of those for whom you pray. Put some sacrifice into it.

Now, the second step is to get the sense of God as light. If you are in a chapel or church, look toward the altar or the cross on the altar. This helps to focus your attention Godward. If you are in some other place, close your eyes and think of God in terms of light. His purpose is always full of light. God is light and in him there is no darkness at all. Into that light, bring Tom, Harry, Emily or the person you are praying for. Don't ask God anything; don't tell him anything; don't beg him for anything. Just bring the person in thought and imagination and lift him into that light. You are looking away from self and into the love of God.

One great danger in intercessory prayer is the tendency to concentrate on the sick or troubled person. You must look away from the trouble. Look away from the disease or the problem and look up to God. "Your will be done on earth, here and now, as it is being done in heaven." If you make this your habitual attitude, you will see a change in your friend. You do this by an act of your will. You hold him in God's presence. Or, if you wish to express it in a different way, you bring your friend by prayer into the Presence of Jesus that God may take care of him. "Hallelujah! For the Lord our God the almighty reigns." (Rev. 19:6). God is good and only good, and the only authentic picture we see of God is in Jesus Christ. The God we worship is the God Jesus preached.

I once heard this described by another person as something like taking a plant out of a cold, dark, damp cellar and lifting it up onto a windowsill where the light of the sun could shine upon it. You well know the difference it made in the plant. It could then live and grow and produce flowers. Don't hold your friend in a thought-cellar or imagination-cellar of darkness, gloom, disease and depression. Lift him into the light. That in itself is a genuine intercession.

Your next step is to try to see the person as God wants him to be. That is not exactly easy. You may have to take an intermediate step. See him as you would like him to be. Get a mental picture of him at his best. You still do not need to ask God. Deep prayer is communion between you and God. This will be a quiet exercise for your imagination. God uses your imagination. With his help, it becomes creative. See Tom cured of his addictions. See Emily recuperating in the hospital. See the nurses, the doctors, the physiotherapists as agents of God's healing power restoring her to health. See God working, bringing perfection out of imperfection, order out of disorder, ease out of disease, peace out of turbulence.

Now, take an additional step. Identify your desire for that person with God's desire. "O God, I identify my will for Emily's recovery with your will for Emily's recovery. I identify my desire for Tom with your desire for his complete wholeness, complete control. I identify my wish for Harry's recovery with your perfect will for his health.

Now, sum up your prayer in an act of thanksgiving. Give thanks because you know that the work of God is being done. "Into your hands, O Lord, I commit this, your child, and I leave him in your presence and I thank you for the light of healing power that is shining upon him, or upon her at this moment."

You need not repeat this whole procedure every day. But you do just keep them committed, hold them in the light consciously. You might say, "O, Lord, I leave Emily in your presence, and I thank you for the benefit she has received in just this last day and night." Something like that. You need follow no set form. Be natural about it. Use your own words.

Then, it is good to have some contact with the person you are praying for. Bring them a little help. Increase their morale by saying a word of encouragement to lift them up a bit. Take them a little pamphlet. There are good ones. Add to your prayer this personal ministry.

Don't try to include too many people in your intercessions just at first. It is better to start with one than with sixteen. In this chapter we have been holding three people at least in our thought and imagination: Tom, Harry and Emily. As you grow in intercession, God will lay people on your heart from time to time. When such an urge comes, don't put it off. Just learn to keep looking Godward and taking people with you.

Some Techniques for Prayer Groups

In a prayer group the emphasis is naturally on prayer. Prayer is cultivating the presence of God. If you are cultivating the presence of God, it is more important for you to hear what God says than for God to hear what you say. After a period of quiet realization of his presence, start with words from the Bible. Why? Because that is his word to us. You need not always follow the same pattern. Vary it, but focus the attention on God and his Word first.

If you have a strong group, one person should not always take the leadership. Don't feel that because you are the leader, you ought to conduct all the meetings. Prepare a person ahead of time by asking in advance that she lead the meeting. One of the greatest proofs of leadership is to create leaders. An unpardonable sin of leadership is to make oneself indispensable. Look to God for a right judgment in all things. You have the presence of the Holy Spirit of God, the spirit of wisdom, always available. A right judgment comes from an educated conscience, an educated consciousness, an educated life (in a spiritual sense) that can quickly get a flash of God's "yes!" Don't despise or discount common sense, but sometimes you have to have uncommon common sense, and especially when you are trying to help people.

As in individual prayer, bear in mind for your group that when you are praying for others, you must look at God first. The great curse of all intercession work is the natural disposition to look at the trouble. One day a list of prayer requests was handed to me, and I want you to try to imagine the effect of a list like this on the faith of a person newly come into the Christian life. You have invited him to come to the prayer group and he is going to help you pray for people. This is the list:

James – cancer!
Mary – tumor of the throat!
Mabel – arthritis!
Walter – multiple sclerosis!

This is just the beginning of the list. The rest is like it. The young Christian thinks to himself: "What do you want me to do with all that? Pray for them?" Can't you imagine the consternation? How in the world is a young Christian, or any Christian(!) going to be able to tackle a bunch of requests like that. All they see is just a name and a terrible disease. In some prayer groups, these names are presented and a prayer something like this is offered for them: "O God, bless these people and help them according to their need." It is better than nothing, perhaps, but it is not nearly good enough.

If you have one hundred requests for prayer and if fifty of them are classed as medically incurable, and if you have fifteen minutes to pray for those people, you will do better to take ten minutes of that time to get a marvelous sense of God's immediate presence and glory and truth and adequacy. If we would just take more time to cultivate a sense of the presence of God, realize that Jesus Christ is the great, ever-present reality and not just a person in history, if we would steep ourselves in the glorious promises of God, then in the next five minutes we could do more bona fide praying for health for others than we could do in two hours by the old method – "O God, we know how terrible this condition is! We know the anguish this person is suffering! In your mercy, please do something to relieve this agony." You know that's old-fashioned. We just don't pray that way today. I am not trying to draw a caricature and God knows I'm not making fun of praying people, but what good is it if we give a long recital of human woes? By the time we get through, we are too exhausted to pray at all. That is not the way.

If you have many requests for prayer in your prayer group, divide them up at the close of the meeting. Don't ask everyone to pray in detail for every request. One prayer group tunes in together at seven o'clock every morning. They take a few minutes off, no matter what they are doing, and pray for the people who have expressed a need. It is just a quick, flash prayer. But we need people who will take real time for intercession and lift people up to God in prayer one by one.

Get reports from time to time on the people for whom you are praying. One prayer group had had fifteen names on its list for some time but had made no investigation. When they were asked to find out about those for whom they had been praying, they found that several were entirely well, a large number showed improvement and two had died. We need a method of keeping track of those for whom we are praying and thanksgiving for answered prayer should be a part of every meeting. In fact, "let your requests be made known to God with thanksgiving."

I once heard of a Christian Science practitioner who was very good. One of his clients brought in a request for prayer, a person who had asked for help through Christian Science. He read the little card which contained a terrible recital of suffering and disease. He said to himself (not meaning to be quoted, of course), "Well, this is beyond me. I can't do a thing about it. I'll just have to leave it to divine mind." The person recovered! Why? Because he left it to divine mind. He didn't do anything about it. Can you learn from that? Instead of divine mind, put whatever you call God. You have a case that is hard to pray for. Well, just be quiet a little while and leave it with the heavenly Father. You have a better prayer in that than the old-fashioned one mentioned above.

The prayer group, or the intercessor, is the point of contact between the heavenly Father and his resources and the needy person for whom we pray.

I was told that experiments were under way in California looking toward the cure of cancer through the use of atomic energy.[1] It is in its initial stages and no report has been issued by the medical profession, but a friend tells me that they are getting many cures. Sheer energy, an invisible force – to cure cancer! And yet, we think it is incredible that Jesus could cure physical diseases with the word of his mouth or the touch of his hand. It is coming. If you don't know what else to do, tell Jesus the problem and leave it there. And remember that your words must exercise faith. They can express faith. Watch your words. "By your words you shall be justified and by your words you shall be condemned." Jesus joyfully accepts our faith and takes us up on it but it must be faith!

---

[1]This was written about 1953.

Why is Healing Sometimes Delayed?

In conducting healing missions, we sometimes have periods for questions and answers. This question has occasionally been raised: "When we pray for healing, we sometimes have to wait a long time. Can anything be done about that?" It is important to remember that God is no respecter of *persons*, but he is a respecter of *conditions*. If people go on thinking negative thoughts, eating the wrong foods, meeting the wrong people, doing the wrong kind of work, and still pray for healing, they may not receive it. The conditions are wrong. I must pray that God will show me the right conditions and give me the faith, the courage and the perseverance to make the conditions right so that he can heal me. Sometimes you must wait while tremendous changes go on in your bodies or in your hearts. Be patient. While you are waiting, make the conditions different. Thousands of arthritic, rheumatic, and diabetic patients are staying that way because they will eat the food they like instead of the food that is good for them.

Or think for a moment about the person who has a nervous breakdown. A Christian should not have a nervous breakdown. A psychologist made the statement, "Every nervous breakdown is a moral breakdown." By that he did not mean that a particular commandment had been broken. He meant a breakdown in morale. A man lowers his standards. Instead of adjusting himself to conditions, he lets conditions get the better of him. He succumbs to the pressure of the hectic life he lives. A nervous breakdown means that the nerves and the emotions have been carrying too heavy a load, and so, in order to prevent death, nature steps in and makes us take an enforced rest which is sometimes very unpleasant. The sovereign remedy for a nervous breakdown is meditation – deliberate, intelligent, continuous, day-by-day meditation. We must pray out of it, not in the sense of petitioning God, but by the prayer of listening, the prayer of affirmation, the prayer of silence, the prayer of dwelling, upon God – that is what will bring release from the stress that causes nervous breakdown. There is no shortcut. People will take pills, but often they won't take ten minutes time daily to wait on God. The latter would do twelve times more good than a pill.

Is Healing Always God's Will?

Then the question is raised about Jesus' prayer in the garden of Gethsemane. Are there times when it is not God's will to heal and when we should pray, "Let what you want be done." "Let what you want be done." is one of the most misunderstood prayers in the Bible. Our Lord's prayer in Gethsemane has nothing whatsoever to do with the healing of the sick. You don't take that prayer into a sick room. That prayer had to do with the sin-burden of the whole world. Jesus was taking upon himself the sins of the whole world. You have never done that and you will never have to do that. It is done. Jesus has once for all taken the sins of the world upon himself – that colossal, incredible burden of sorrow and anguish – and it weighted him down so that he almost fell under the weight of it and cried out in his extremity, "Father, if it be possible, let this cup pass from me. Nevertheless, let what you want be done."

It is almost blasphemy for a person with a disease today to think that the bearing of a pathological condition is part of Gethsemane. Yet, some people get emotional satisfaction out of saying, "Oh, well, this is my Gethsemane. May God's will be done." That is a false picture. It is an unjust transposition of events. You are not passing through Gethsemane because you are dying of cancer. You are suffering because the law of God has been broken somewhere. Maybe you had nothing to do with it. Maybe it is due to any one of a number of things, but don't say it is Gethsemane. It is not. Disease will always yield to the perfect will of God. Disease is the enemy. Jesus regarded disease as the work of the devil. In one of the Apostle Peter's recorded discourses, he says, "How God anointed Jesus of Nazareth with the Holy Ghost and with power;

...he went about doing good and healing all who were oppressed by the devil, for God was with him. We are witnesses to all that he did..." (Acts 10:38-39).

You may speak about the sweet uses of adversity. That is all right. You may say that you have learned some valuable lessons through pain. That is all right, too. I don't doubt it. You may say that in some of the great troubles of life that have fallen upon you, you have built up character. I'll believe that. But don't say that loathsome disease is God's will for mankind. The doctor has known all along that disease is an evil thing. Yet, out of our foggy thinking and our ambiguous theology, we have sometimes gone to the sick room and tried to comfort a sick person by saying, "Well, no doubt, this is God's will. Just be patient under the hand of God!

Well, what is the hand of God? If you are the father of a child and you want to educate that child or even to punish him, would you give him a disease? Would you give your child a disease to punish him? You would be a devil in human form if you did. Yet some of our theology has attributed that very thing to God. It is assumed that disease is inevitable and unavoidable, and therefore should be accepted with a certain degree of resignation. The prayer of resignation must be superseded by the prayer of enthusiastic cooperation. So much depends on how you say, "Let what you want be done." What is in your mind when you say those words? What is your tone of voice when you say them? "Your healing will be accomplished?" Or, "I accept this illness, this disease, this failure, this misery, this fear as my just punishment for my sins?" Take your choice. Jesus said, "Let what you want be done on earth as it is done in heaven." Is there any disease in heaven? Any surgical operations in heaven? Any schizophrenia in heaven? Any inferiority complexes in heaven? You know there are not. "Let what you want be done on earth as it is done in heaven."

If God Wills Healing, Why Do People Die?

"But," someone raises the question, "perhaps the time has come for that person to die?" Death is never God's will. Transition from this plane to another plane is God's will. Jesus said, "Whosoever liveth and believeth in me shall never die." (John 11:26 [KJV]). Again he says, "Verily, verily, I say unto you, If a man keep my saying he shall never see death." (John 8:51 [KJV]). These sayings preceded by "verily, verily" are always powerful. We say that this means that when we get to heaven we never die. That is not what Jesus said. Death by disease is not God's will, but eighty per cent go out of this world through disease because of the accumulated disobedience of mankind. But

God did not create us to die through disease. God meant us to spend a certain length of time on this plane, learn our lessons, do our work, fulfill our vocation and then be translated to another plane where we can do a much higher work. It is nonsense to say that we have to have tuberculosis or cancer in order to go on to that higher plane. It is contrary to the teaching of Jesus. There is not one case where Jesus acquiesces in the death of any one person by disease or by accident. Yet we assume it to be true.

"If a man keep my saying he shall never see death," Jesus said. The trouble is – we don't keep his sayings. We just read them affectionately! We keep a lot of other things that are negative in our minds. There is a wonderful book entitled ***Intelligent Living*** by Robert B. H. Bell. It is a study of the commandments of Jesus – not the Ten Commandments of the Old Testament, but the commandments of Jesus, the things he told his disciples to do. There are thirty-three of them. As you study them, you will begin to see why only a minority of professing Christians get anywhere with the real hard work of the Christian life. It takes perseverance to "keep his saying," but the reward is glorious.

Look a little more closely at this saying of Jesus. Jesus said, "If a man keep my saying he shall never see death." Jesus did not say that the body would not die. He said that the man would not see death. A person may say, "Well, nobody ever demonstrated that."

Yes, thousands of people have! Following a statement of this kind in one of my sermons, two medical doctors talked with me. Both agreed with me. One of them said, "Dozens of my patients never see death." He said, "Their spirit is gone twenty minutes, thirty minutes, sometimes more than an hour before the body dies." They are gone! They don't see death! They say also that the actual spirit passes usually in peace. Usually the soul goes on without witnessing the death of the body. So, you see, there is some approximation at least in medical science to the words of Jesus. We must stretch our minds, stretch our imaginations and seek to measure up to the attitude Jesus had toward death.

What if People Resent Prayer?

Then this question is sometimes asked by members of prayer groups: "Suppose people resent your praying for them?" We pray for many people who never know or suspect for one minute that they are being prayed for. You can pray for anyone, with or without his consent. It is wonderful to have cooperation, but it is not absolutely essential. Don't ask a person's cooperation in prayer unless you expect to get it. If a person is belligerent, aggressive or argumentative, just pray quietly without argument. Sometimes an individual will feel that you are judging him and that causes him to have a negative reaction. If you have the urge to pray, or if somebody asks you to pray, the less you dwell on the shortcomings of the patient, the better. If you can get the cooperation of the patient, however, by all means do so.

Visiting the Sick

Or again, the question is raised, "What techniques should we use in our relationships to sick people – we who belong to prayer groups?" If you really want to help sick people and pray with them, you must carefully discriminate in your own mind between want on the one hand and need on the other hand. There is a world of difference. Some sick people want sympathy more than anything else. Bless their hearts! I know their situation is difficult. But they want to be pitied; they want to be coddled; they want to be spoiled. They want attention lavished on them. This is a natural human impulse. Not all sick people are like that, of course, but many of them are. We sometimes make the mistake of thinking that we must help them by giving them exactly the thing they want – petting, coddling, listening to their tales of woe. There is nothing that is more of a sheer luxury to a sick person than to find somebody kind enough and patient enough to sit down and listen to his tale of woe. The telling of that tale of woe does give a momentary relief. There is an emotional relief that comes from it. But do not assume that that is a cure, for very frequently it is not. Jesus went like an arrow to the need of the patient. He did say, "What do you want me to do for you?" to arouse the will of the one to whom he ministered, but that is quite different from catering to his wants. There is an altruistic love that unerringly, almost intuitively, goes to the needs, to the very heart of another person's need, and discounts his superficial wants and wishes. If you are too sympathetic, you are not a good intercessor. It is a fault to be sympathetic to the point of confirming people in their negative conditions. They need healing and they need love, but love itself must be disciplined.

When the centurion came to Jesus to request healing for his sick servant, Jesus instantly replied, "I will come and heal him." But the centurion's faith led him to say, "It will not be necessary. You are a man with authority. I am a man with authority. But I am also under authority. When I tell my servant to do something, I don't worry any more about it. I know it is done. And if you say that my servant is to be healed, I shall know it is all right. You don't have to come." Jesus had never met a person with such an extraordinary degree of faith.

On another occasion when a nobleman begged Jesus to come and heal his son, Jesus said in effect, "It isn't necessary for me to come. You go home. It will be all right. If you go home now, you will show by that action that you have faith in my word, and that is all I ask."

The centurion was humble enough and had faith enough not to ask for such attention. We need not offer long, extemporaneous prayers even for sick people. Often, there is much more faith in the brief petition of the centurion, "Only speak the word and my servant will be healed." (Matthew 8:8). We must be careful, however, not to criticize other people because they do not measure up to what we think is the perfect standard. And there may, of course, be times when considerable attention is needed. As you seek to grow in the spirit of Jesus, God will let you know the degree of attention that is needed. It is part of getting a right judgment in all things and comes through prayer. It is so easy with sick people to say just the words they would like to hear, the words that flatter their ego, or minimize their faults to the nth degree. But it is better to have a great love for them, and then to speak the truth in love. All our prayers would be answered if we would just continually live in the consciousness that "the divine *yes* has sounded in him, for in him is the *yes* that affirms all the promises of God."

O God, may your peace, your perfect poise be established in our hearts. We pray that our eyes may be opened to see the truth as it is in Jesus. May we have the mind of Christ and learn all the lessons you want to teach us, for the kingdom, the power and the glory are yours, now and forever. Amen.

Questions

1. On page 190, Banks writes, "Discipline is the process of becoming a disciple and it takes perseverance, persistence, an intelligent indoctrination in the teaching of Jesus."

   How long have you worked with the healing of others and what have you found to be the most difficult part of that? What does "an intelligent indoctrination" mean to you?

2. "An intercessor is one who prays for others." (p. 199) How does the author suggest that we handle all the requests we receive for prayer (p. 193-198)?

3. What are the common mistakes of prayer groups and what is suggested as a remedy?

4. A person is sick and asks you to pray for her/him. You clearly see that the sickness is being caused by the way they treat their body. What do you say?

5. What suggestions does the author have for visiting the sick?

XII

THE SECRETS OF DISCIPLESHIP

THE STORY is told of a dear old lady who was very quiet and devout, and who had a prayer that she said every night and many times a day. "O God, take away the cobwebs from my eyes!" Another lady who was living with her and who got tired of hearing this same prayer over and over said, "Why don't you pray, 'O God, kill that spider!'" Get rid of the spider and there won't be any more cobwebs! We deal with *effects* when we ought to deal with *causes*. We pray like that. We pray about the thing that we see which is an *effect*, and we fail to get down to *real causes*.

In regard to this ministry of healing, why don't we have more success – more power – in our healing work? My answer can be put into one sentence: Because we are not initiated Christians! Are you just a Christian, or are you an initiated Christian? Some twenty-six million people in this country belong to secret orders.

There are dozens of secret organizations here in the United States and they all thrive. They are getting new members all the time. Why do so many people join these secret orders? They want to be initiated. They want to be on the "inside." They want to have secrets that other people don't have. I am not critical of that. Some of these orders give us a lot to live up to. But its object is to initiate its members into a deeper understanding of life.

Now, Christian initiation is very much like that. Christian initiation is meant to introduce us, to lead us into a deeper quality of living in Jesus Christ. There are some people who become dissatisfied with being just ordinary, mediocre Christians. Thank God if you have that divine discontent! The greatest problem of the Christian Church lies in the large number of mediocre members that it has. Dr. Sammy Jones, years ago, put it in a very clever way. He said, "The Church is so inoculated with the dead germs of Christianity, that it has become immune to the real thing." By an *initiated Christian* I mean one who has emerged from mediocrity and is headed toward that status that the New Testament mentions as becoming "kings and priests unto God."

Don't be afraid of the phrase "kings and priests." A king is a man who *can*. It suggests power and the early kings were men who "could," men who were exalted above their fellows because they demonstrated power and achievement. Priests were men who could represent their brothers before God, men who could speak for God, to God and with God. It is the destiny of every Christian to become "a king and a priest unto God." Few of us have that degree of initiation.

It has meant a great deal to me to think this matter of initiation through and the people who have thought it through with me are the strongest members in The International Order of St. Luke. The International Order of St. Luke does not consist of superior people, but it does consist of people many of whom, at least, have achieved some degree of initiation. It is a group of men and women who seek deeper initiation in order that God can use them in the promotion of divine healing in the churches and in the world. We know by our study, our prayer, our fellowship and our sharing that this doesn't just happen. Why is it that many people pray for healing and nothing happens? It is because we don't pray right. James says in his Epistle, "You want something and do not have it... You ask and do not receive, because you ask wrongly." (James 4:2-3). We have not learned how to pray. We need initiation even in prayer. We certainly need initiation for this healing ministry. The members of the International Order of St. Luke do not claim to be any better than other people. We are seeking. We are opening doors. We are finding new techniques for living, learning, loving, praying and healing. We are helping each other to achieve that larger initiation which is possible.

When I was at Milton Abbey, I was wearing my blue cassock and a young priest who was with me said to me one day, very naively, "Father, if I join the International Order of St. Luke, can I wear a cassock like yours?" Two or three days later a nurse said to me, "Oh, I want one of those little gold pins. Could I join the International Order of St. Luke and wear one of those little gold pins?" The cassock and the pin are not signs of spiritual aristocracy. I think it is a great help in the healing ministry to wear a color other than black, but these are only outward evidences of things much more important. I covet for all my readers the experience of *being*, not *appearing* initiated Christians.

Now, what is the essence of it? There is a whole chapter in the Bible on initiation. It is the tenth chapter of the Gospel of Luke. That whole chapter from start to finish is a study in initiation. I used to exclude the story of the good Samaritan, but that story is an integral part of it. The good Samaritan, you know, had something that the priest and Levite didn't have. They were ordained: they were appointed: they held office; they were highly regarded by their neighbors: but they did not have what that poor man by the roadside needed. The good Samaritan did have it. You may have heard the story of the Sunday School teacher who wanted to determine whether the boys in her class really understood this story, so she inquired, "Why did the priest and the Levite pass by on the other side?" One little boy thought a minute and then said, "Well, they saw the man had already been robbed." One tragic aspect of organized religion is that it sometimes appears to be more concerned with what it is getting from people than with what it is giving them. The Christian Church should be primarily concerned with what she has to give. When this desire is primary, God will see that she does not lack anything. God will take care of her needs, and of our needs individually too when we take this attitude.

In the tenth chapter of the Gospel of Luke, we see Jesus sending out seventy disciples. They were laity with very little experience. They had no theological training such as we have today. But do you not see that Jesus would not be foolish enough to send out seventy disciples to carry his message, to represent him, unless they had first been initiated? He had given them some preparation. Luke does not tell us what their preparation was but as you read the Gospel you see that they had been with him. The personal, intimate revelations he made to them represented a most profound initiation. Suppose I were to take seventy people out of an average church today, out of any

Sunday morning service and say to them, "Now, folks, you will have to go out on a six-day missionary journey – proclaim the Gospel, heal the sick, cast out demons, cleanse lepers, and if necessary, even raise the dead." Do you suppose they would do it? Can you imagine the way they would look at me? Yet they would be members of regularly organized Christian Churches! What would be the difference between the seventy and those I would select? The ones Jesus sent out were initiated – that is the difference.

This initiation is something that any of you may have if you want it. Jesus would like to include you. He wants you on the inside of this movement. He does not want you to be just a nominal church member. He wants you to be dynamic. You can't rush out in five minutes on a sudden impulse to proclaim the kingdom of heaven, but when you are initiated, Jesus will send you out. You will be humble about it. You won't do a great deal of talking about your qualifications. You don't talk about the secrets of your order, do you? Aren't you pledged to secrecy about certain things? There are times when Jesus says, "Tell no one." There are some experiences in the Christian life that are solemnly individual. They are between you and God. It is at your peril that you tell those out. "Do not throw your pearls before swine." The trouble with so many of us is that we haven't any pearls to cast! We ought to have pearls. We ought to know where to keep them and what to do with them. Jesus Christ has incredible riches to give his followers. In the Middle Ages they used to put this somewhat mystical idea in three words, "All for All!" The mystic gives his all to God and in return he receives God's all – all he is able to receive.

The thought of surrendering your all to God and receiving God's all may seem a rather daring one, but why acquiesce in spiritual mediocrity! I went to a summer camp in California a number of years ago and it was attended mostly by young people. I learned some things at that camp. There was a very bright girl there. They called her "Happy Morgan." She was about twenty years old, attractive and full of vitality. I was in one of her group meetings when she was talking on personal problems. The group was made up of people who were her own age – teenage and a little older. She put this terrific challenge to them – "Have you surrendered the inevitability of mediocrity?" You would be surprised how many people have not. We assume that we are going to be mediocre. We never did get much education. We haven't much family background. What was good enough for my father is good enough for me, and it wasn't too good! We acquiesce in mediocrity. We have never glimpsed the idea that we might be giants, that we might be over-comers. We have not read or understood those early chapters of the Revelation where Jesus, through the spirit, talked in terms of overcoming and pronounced benedictions and beatitudes on those who do overcome. Have you surrendered the inevitability of spiritual mediocrity? Can you picture yourself as giving your all and receiving God's all? Getting this picture is the secret preparation for initiation.

But how will you know that you are initiated? Here are some questions which will help you to know.

1. What did Jesus mean when he said, "I thank you, Father, Lord of heaven and earth, because you have hidden these things from the wise and the intelligent and have revealed them to infants." (Luke 10:21). In Oriental languages the word *"infant"* is also the word used for "initiate." An initiate is being inducted into a higher realm of consciousness. Into that higher realm he comes first as a baby. You are an *infant* when you join a lodge – a baby member of the order. But you are still an initiate. You will go on to higher planes and higher achievements as circumstances permit. I have joined five secret orders in the course of my ministry, but I do not know any sentence of any secret order that impresses me as much as one that Jesus spoke to this little group of initiates. I would gladly give any privilege or benefit I have received from all these five put together in exchange for this one. "Then turning to the disciples,

Jesus said to them privately..." (Luke 10:23). This was not a public utterance to the man on the street. The man on the street would not understand these words. A large proportion of church members do not understand them. But the initiate or the one who is ready for initiation does understand them. Jesus said, "Blessed are the eyes which see the things that you see; for I tell you that many prophets and kings have desired to see those things which you see and have not seen them, and to hear those things which you hear, and have not heard them." Have you seen what they saw? Have you heard what they heard? Could Jesus say those words about you? Remember that those disciples proved that they were initiates by doing the work Jesus sent them out to do. Nothing is more humbling to me, nothing keeps me in place better than the realization of the discrepancy between the fruits of my ministry today and the fruits of the ministry of those disciples . And yet, there is enough fruitage to know that the results come when we fulfill the conditions. The plan of Jesus for his church in the world has not been changed in more than nineteen centuries. The program of Jesus for the twentieth century is substantially what we find it to be in the four gospels. The working out of that program still proceeds very much as it did in the acts of the apostles. There is still that conflict between the world's standards of success on one hand and Jesus' standard of success on the other side. The church has too often compromised. The church has sometimes borrowed too much of the technique of the world, but the real church, the church within the church, the true church of Jesus which is back of all the denominations, still establishes its credentials by bringing forth the results that Jesus said they would produce. Those who exercise a real healing ministry have to be real Christians. You don't get healing results from just tinkering with the Christian faith. That is why a healing prayer group should be a group of real seekers who want to go all the way with God, who want to know the real commandments of Jesus and keep them, and who want to establish a rapport, a harmony, a mutual love and understanding that you don't often find.

2. Why were these disciples given this personal initiation by the Lord himself? One reasonable answer is that he wanted to qualify them for the highest outgoing service in changing lives and healing souls and bodies and ushering in the new kingdom. He wants to do the same thing today. He is asking you whether you are qualified, ready, prepared to engage in this tremendous enterprise of changing lives, of bringing healing to souls and bodies of men, and of hastening the coming of the kingdom of God on earth.

The ninth chapter of the Gospel of Luke serves as an introduction to the tenth. Read what it says about the sending out of the twelve. The instructions to the twelve were very similar to the instructions to the seventy. We are told that Jesus called the twelve together. Without doubt the seventy were with him a great deal too. You can't be with Jesus without learning the deeper lessons of discipleship. Jesus placed healing among the major activities of this ministry. It is an essential, vital, fundamental and indispensable part of it.

You frequently hear the words quoted, "You will know the truth and the truth will make you free." Those words are quoted as a slogan. But there is a condition attached to them, and unless that condition is met, they are not true. The condition is, "If you continue in my word, you are truly my disciples." Then, it follows that, "You will know the truth and the truth will make you free." So Jesus brings us to the status of genuine discipleship.

3. What are the mutual relationships of those who have achieved any degree of initiation? Those who are candidates for initiation attract each other. They are traveling the same path. They need reinforcement. They seek fellowship. They need mutual strengthening. There is established between them a bond, a much deeper relationship than that of blood.

Let me take an illustration from the Bible. Jesus is in a house teaching. The place is crowded. There comes a knock on the door. "Is Jesus of Nazareth inside?...

Well, his mother and his brothers are out here and they want him." Jesus stops talking and looks around. This is not the time to chat with members of his family. With dignity, but not with anger, he says, "Who is my mother? Who are my brothers?" Nobody answers. So Jesus answers his own question. His disciples are sitting together near him and he points to them, saying, "Whoever does the will of my Father in heaven is my brother and sister and mother."

When Jesus hung on the cross, his disciples had forsaken him and fled. Two remained – his mother and John, the beloved disciple. They stayed with him. They were very lonely. They knew they would soon be bereaved. They did not know all the joys of the resurrection that were coming. They saw only the terrible reality of the cross and the separation. Jesus said to John, and perhaps with his eyes, he pointed to Mary, "Here is your mother." Was Mary the mother of John? Naturally, no; spiritually, yes, but the spiritual relation was more important than the domestic relationship and it still is. And then, he looked at Mary, and with his eyes pointed to John, said, "Woman, here is your son." Thereby Jesus created new relationships. He is doing it all the time.

I don't care to have every Tom, Dick and Harry calling me "brother." This brother and sister business used promiscuously doesn't mean a thing. But there are real relationships of brother and sister among the initiated.

If it is limited to those who are in the very deepest sense brothers and sisters in Christ, then it is wonderful, but to use the terms without the reality smacks of insincerity. I love to call certain people sister or brother, but I want it to come from a recognition of something that calls out that expression, a mutual recognition, a reciprocity on the spiritual plane.

I have a brother now in Afghanistan. He really lives in Washington but is temporarily in Afghanistan. He is quite as much a brother to me as any brother in the flesh could be. I have another brother in New York, a medical doctor who is simply a brother whom I met and recognized on the spiritual plane. He is considerably younger than I am, but he is my brother. I have sisters also. I have a daughter whose natural father was very brutal to her as a child, sadistic, horrible. She never knew what a real father meant and we were accidentally, as people say, brought together in a mission. She told me her story and I said, "Well, you need another father." She said, "I wish you would be my father." I said, "Well, I certainly will." I have had great joy in being a father to that girl who never knew what any real fatherly attitude was. God has all sorts of relationships for you if you will take them his way, and on his terms and on a spiritual plane and as part of the enterprise of the kingdom of God on earth. These are among the rewards of initiation.

4. Have you a personal theology? You say, "I'm not interested in theology." Very few people are. But the Son will reveal to you as a Christian initiate the true nature of the Father, and the Father will reveal the true nature of the Son. That revelation will give you your personal theology. You don't get it out of books. And that is one of the rewards of initiation.

5. Have you a share in the greater works of Jesus? Don't say, "That is for the clergy. " Nonsense! Jesus said, "The works that I do shall you do also and greater works than these shall you do because I go to the Father." You may pray that somehow God in his inscrutable wisdom will bring the healing ministry into the Church but it will take a long time – if you do nothing more than pray. What he needs are initiated Christians, committed Christians. These people do not advertise themselves. Initiates don't. You don't talk about your initiation. You talk about Jesus. The greater works will be demonstrated in the Church when a few people here and there have accepted the responsibility that Jesus has given them.

Dr. Kunkel, a psychiatrist in Los Angeles, author of several books, has some most important things to say in ***Creation Continues***. It is a book on the Gospel of Matthew written from the standpoint of a psychiatrist. He has not had training in theology. He says, "When you read the Gospel of Matthew, you read through to chapter eight before you get any miracles." Why? The commentaries don't tell you, but Dr. Kunkel does! You don't get any miracles till chapter eight because chapters five, six and seven are the Sermon on the Mount. Those chapters contain the principles of initiation into the Christian life. Until you have accepted the principles of initiation, the Sermon on the Mount, you are not ready to understand miracles and you are certainly not ready to work miracles. Have you a share in the greater works?

6. Do you know the meaning of divine love? Divine love is real love but not mere sentiment. The Bible has four words that are translated by the English word "love": "*eros*" meaning human love, the love of a man for a woman, not exclusively sex love but including that; "*philia*," which means brotherly love; "*caritas*" which refers to altruism; and "*agape*" which means divine love. It is the last kind of love which Jesus had for his disciples. Read the 13th, 14th, 15th and 16th chapters of the Gospel of John and see how Jesus uses the word "love." The love of God became vocal in Jesus. The grand climax is in the last verse of the 17th chapter of this gospel. Do you know what this means? A paraphrased quote from the poet Samuel Taylor Coleridge goes, "Those pray best who love best all things both great and small,"[1]

---

[1] Coleridge, The Ancient Mariner, Part vii:
"He prayeth best who loveth best
All things both great and small;
For the dear God who loveth us,
He made and loveth all."

Meditate on it. Poets come nearer to the heart of God sometimes than do theologians.

7. **Do you understand the mutual dependence of love and prayer?** I learned the relationship between love and prayer by going to the summer Camps Farthest Out Camps. I ought to have learned it in the church, but somehow I did not. Love makes you pray and prayer is activated by love. You cannot pray successfully without love and you cannot love powerfully without praying. The mutual relationship of love and prayer is one of the fruits of initiation. It is one of the things that you learn when you know the secrets of Jesus. The love of Christ made these early initiates powerful in prayer. The men and women I know today who do good in the world as individuals are people who have great love, in whom the love of God is made manifest, in whom his love becomes vocal, audible, approachable. When our prayers seem feeble, they need reinforcement. They need activating, This comes through the love of God. It is when the love of Christ compels us that we shall be able really to pray.

We are looking for the approval of Jesus himself. We are looking for a contemporary experience of the gospel of Christ, of the healing of Christ and of the power of Christ. We are looking for the coming of his kingdom right in our own vicinity, right in our own community, right in our own church of which we are already a part.

The International Order of St. Luke is for those who want to take these further degrees of initiation. Humbly, on our knees, we ask God to take us and use us and initiate us into those further stages of Christian experience that will enable us to be effectively employed in this redemptive ministry. The International Order of St. Luke is for men and women, laity and clergy, all whom God calls to the full ministry of Jesus Christ.

Every candidate for the International Order of St. Luke is expected to have a vocation. What do I mean by a vocation? It is not just something to join if you are mildly interested in the study of Christian healing. You must be prepared to do something about this healing work. There are, of course, many vocations within the ministry of healing. Doctors, who want to serve God through their medical practice, nurses, hospital visitors, leaders of prayer groups, active workers in prayer and intercession groups, ministers, parish visitors, people who work with mental patients, people who work with children – all, in fact, who are offering themselves to God with the intention of following Jesus in his healing ministry – are eligible to membership in the International Order of St. Luke. Membership in this order brings you into a wonderful fellowship of love and service. Many have testified to the blessing they have found in it.

Let me give you one further illustration of what I mean by *vocation*. I had been holding a healing mission in an eastern city. The congregation was made up of cultured, appreciative and attentive people, but they did not want to do anything about putting their faith into practice. They just wanted to listen. There was no response at all when I put the challenge of the International Order of St. Luke before them. No one apparently wished to be inducted. As I was leaving the church, a woman approached me rather timidly and reluctantly and said that she would like to join the International Order of St. Luke. She did not look like a person with a vocation and I had to try and explain to her the requirements for membership in the order. May God forgive me! But I was trying to imagine just what she could do, what kind of service she could render! She smiled and said tentatively, "I'm a helper in a home for old people and I try to bring a little sunshine into their lives!" Of course she was eligible. She was inducted the next day and she is doing a good work of bringing light into the lives of people who might, without her ministry, find life boring and gloomy. You don't know what vocation God might open up for you as you become more willing to let him work through you. The healing ministry will have a new thrill for you when you have a part in it yourself. It is a ministry for the whole Christian Church and every member may have an active share in it.

Let us close our eyes for a moment and open our spiritual eyes. Dear heavenly Father, forgive us because we have talked too much and done too little. Forgive us if we have tried too hard to explain things and given inadequate time to the secret, silent working of your Holy Spirit. Quicken our understanding, arouse our want, our capacity for your supreme divine love. Move us to the point where we give it out joyfully to those who need it. Teach us how to pray with great love. Teach us how to use our ability to love in our prayers. Show us our next steps. Give us grace for a degree of sacrifice. Make us to count the cost of this larger, fuller experience and to pay the price joyfully. Lead us to those people with whom we ought to work and pray. Complete our family relationships on this basis. May there be no lonely, isolated disciples. But may we find that enduring fellowship which you will for your children day by day. Give us the grace to take this message into our own church and our own community, not aggressively but animated by the love of Jesus and the wisdom of the Spirit, for the kingdom and the power and the glory are yours for ever and ever. Amen.

Questions

1. Banks maintains that there is a gap between the person who attends church and the one who is committed to belonging to Christ. What can we do to help people become more committed to following Jesus' practices and directives to his disciples?
2. Read Luke 9. Why do you believe that this applies to Christians today?
3. Where have you experienced the family which God has given you?
4. The author suggests that we read chapters 13, 14, 15, 16, and 17 of John. What ideas seem most important to you?
5. Pray the prayer on page 233.

XIII

THE CONQUEST OF DEATH NOW!

AM ULTIMATE IN THE HEALING MINISTRY

"Very truly, I tell you, whoever keeps my Word will never see death!"

– John 8:51

RESURRECTION is not a date on the calendar, nor can it be understood by any triumphant celebration of Easter Day. The resurrection of Jesus Christ began as an historical event. It is held today as an article of faith by all Christian people. The implications of the first Easter and the whole resurrection teaching of the Church point to Jesus as the conqueror of death. This conquest was not for himself alone but for all who have achieved new life in him. Seventy-five per cent (at least) of Christian believers celebrate this event on one day in the year – they call it Easter and it has become a tremendous festival in many ways. Yet the Church was led by the spirit of truth (actually the spirit of Jesus) to extend this celebration for a period of forty days usually called the Great Forty Days and finding its climax quite logically in Ascensiontide and Pentecost. This period should be marked by a cumulative development in study and devotion. It should be even more powerful than the forty days of Lent which precede Easter. If we need forty days (plus six Sundays) for penitential exercise and cleansing in preparation for Easter, we surely need a similar period to absorb the priceless events in our Lord's life which begin with the rising from the tomb and conclude with the glorious facts of Ascension and Pentecost! If you say in reply that the observance of the great forty days is an obsolete custom of the Church which we have now outgrown, I would reply by begging you to spend ten minutes of quiet devotional study on verses 1-3 of the first chapter of The Acts.

What Are the Convincing Proofs?

It reveals far more than might appear from a quick reading. It would include all the amazing personal manifestations of our Lord after his rising to various individuals and groups. It would include some astounding phrases and promises of our Lord which belong exclusively to this period of gospel history. It would include the discovery that the contents of the three synoptic gospels only give us what Jesus began to "do and teach." The post-resurrection words and actions provide the clue for a more advanced spiritual development than we ever dared to conceive. The example and teaching of Jesus during this period are for the disciples alone – not for the general public (either in his day or in ours).

> In the first book, Theophilus, I wrote about all that Jesus did and taught from the beginning until the day when he was taken up to heaven, after giving instructions through the Holy Spirit to the apostles whom he had chosen. After his suffering he presented himself alive to them by many convincing proofs, appearing to them during forty days and speaking about the kingdom of God.
>
> – Acts 1:1-3

There is a meaning for today in every line of those three verses. Are you actually conversant with "all that Jesus did and taught from the beginning"? Are you acquainted with those "instructions" which Jesus gave through the Holy Spirit? Do you imagine they were only for those particular apostles and disciples? Has he "presented himself alive" to you? Can you bear witness to "many convincing proofs" of final victory over death? Are you familiar with his "speaking about the kingdom of God" which he revealed during those great forty days?

Are you actually conversant with "all that Jesus did and taught"? Are you acquainted with those "commandments" which Jesus gave through the Holy Spirit? Do you imagine they were only for those particular apostles and disciples? Has he "presented himself alive" to you? Can you bear witness to "many convincing proofs" of final victory over death? Are you familiar with the things "about the kingdom of God" which he revealed during those great forty days. These questions are not meant to embarrass you, but merely to arouse you to a genuine quest, a definite seeking for that fuller and more victorious life which he planned for his disciples in every age.

The Fruits of Easter

But above all else we can learn from the great forty days as recorded in the Christian gospels that a genuine victory over death is possible here and now. If we stop regarding the conquest of death as a mere counsel of perfection – a pious hope relegated to the hereafter, and begin to see it as an intrinsic part of Christ's teaching for his followers in all ages, our thinking will become clearer and we may be surprised to see how this idea of victory over death permeates the New Testament scriptures from Matthew to Revelation!

I could quote dozens of scripture verses to establish this thesis, but the briefest statement of the truth here emphasized will be found in the Easter Preface for the Holy Communion Service given on page 78 of the current edition of the ***American Prayer Book***:

> But chiefly are we bound to praise you for the glorious resurrection of your Son Jesus Christ our Lord; for he is the true Paschal Lamb, who was sacrificed for us, and has taken away the sin of the world. By his death he has destroyed death, and by his rising to life again he has won for us everlasting life.

If you don't like liturgies, please remember that these words are fully substantiated by numerous Bible references, which space forbids us to quote here. I hold firmly that a devotional study of the great forty days would produce in us the fruits of the resurrection, and give us the key to Ascension and Pentecost. The cycle of the Christian year is a condensed gospel which we not merely follow, but actually cultivate within ourselves. Let us grasp more firmly the amazing doctrine of Jesus as conqueror of death. "For since death came through a human being, the resurrection of the dead has also come through a human being; for as all die in Adam, even so will all be made alive in Christ." (1 Cor. 15:21-22).

The Words of Jesus

Long before his passion and death, Jesus claimed to be the conqueror of death and used words of incredible force and power, only reduced in efficacy because we have heard them so often. He said: "Very truly, I tell you, whoever keeps my Word will never see death!" (John 8:51). In his recently-published translation of the gospels, J. B. Phillips renders this verse thus: "Believe Me when I tell you that if anybody accepts My words, they will never experience death at all." Frankly this is not the creed of the average professing Christian today! It is so easy to "explain it away." Again Jesus said: "I am the resurrection and the life. Those who believe in me, even thought they die, will live, and everyone who lives and believes in me will never die." (John 11:25-26). Did Jesus mean what he said or must we cloud his meaning with clever metaphors? There is nothing in all our Lord's utterances more striking than his personal aversion to death which breathed through them. Thus it has been said with truth that death is the one natural fact, the one human experience, to which Jesus showed antipathy. Why should he take this attitude? Why should he ignore or discount an incident as unfailing and natural as old age? If he declined to speak of death as death, it was because he saw through it, because he knew its true nature and ever looked on beyond it to that higher and fuller life of which it is supposed to be the portal.

When Jesus is told that the daughter of Jairus is dead he declares she is only asleep. And when the news is brought to him of the death of his friend Lazarus, he put the hated word from him and declared that Lazarus was only "sleeping." He did not change the phrase till the dullness of the disciples compelled him. Similarly, when the young man of Nain, the only son of his mother, was brought to Jesus on the bier ready for burial, Jesus refused to admit any cause for sorrow, any occasion for the demonstrative weeping and wailing that was heard on such occasions. He said to the mother, "Do not weep!" and when he came closer he touched the bier and said to the seemingly dead youth: "Young man, I say to you, rise!" The dead man sat up and began to speak. (Luke 7:12-16).

Is Death Real?

Luke is not given to exaggerations. The story has all the marks of veracity. It produced a deep impression upon the bystanders: "Fear seized all of them: and they glorified God saying, 'A great prophet has risen among us'; and 'God has looked favorably on his people'." (v. 16).

It is clear enough from these three instances of our Lord's close contact with what we call death that he saw so clearly beyond the immediate phenomenon as to discredit the reality of death and to discount its power to disturb the true child of God. He is inculcating a new mode of thought and speech in regard to the close of man's earthly life.

How Does Christ Conquer Death?

Let us go on to discover why it is we may take Jesus literally on these vital words of his. Just as at the grave of Lazarus, our Lord sets himself forth as the guarantee that death is not what it seems, so in the words there employed (John 11:25-26) we find a formula of truth that could still be valid on our lips today. Union with Christ and obedience to him will put us beyond the reach and power of death! Medical friends of mine tell me that the majority of people do not "see death" or "feel death" even today. Long before the body dies (technically speaking) the spirit gently withdraws and is not even present when the body actually expires. Doubtless Jesus meant more than this, but even this limited experience would justify his words for many. Even the word "expire" only means to breathe out, and when used of death it means to breathe out for the last time on this planet. Through Christ life has become a ruling power. He stands in the midst of humanity for an eternal reality, and he came that men might know it and embrace it.

How Can These Things Be?

The resurrection supplies the clue. The same power that could declare freedom from sin – that could say, "Son, your sins are forgiven!" or "Daughter, your faith has made you well; go in peace." and so could bring an actual sense of cleansing and release and renewal...

the same power that could bring sight to the blind and hearing to the deaf, and speech to the dumb, and cleansing to the leper… the same power that made Jesus walk on the waves and multiply the loaves and fishes, and still the tempest… the same power that made him call back Lazarus from the dead (after three days of disintegration)… that took the hand of the daughter of Jairus and exclaimed, "Child, get up!"… that gave back the young man of Nain to his mother, when the body was just about to be buried. That power, I say, is the power that raised up Jesus Christ from the dead and showed him alive to his disciples!

A truly Christian death is a supernatural experience. This girl and the two young men just cited doubtless grew to years of maturity and finally reached the end of their earthly pilgrimages. But I can imagine them (each one) at the end of the journey, recalling the great experience, reciting many times the life-giving words of Jesus, and so drifting into blissful unconsciousness and waking up in eternal life. That "blissful unconsciousness" is no pretty phrase. It occurs usually hours before the fact of physical death arrives – certainly quite a while before – and it has been the experience of thousands of humble Christians, not just the heroes of the faith. As we become ready to receive it, there is a still higher experience for us, something comparable to that of Moses, of

Enoch, of Elijah, who, in each case, made the transition without illness or disease or senility. Of Enoch it is simply written: "He was no more, for God took him" – he literally "walked with God." (Gen. 5:24). Finally, and for ourselves today, "The blood of our Lord Jesus Christ keep you in everlasting life!" We shall find in that sacred blood the antidote for death. And in his sacred body, received by faith (sacramentally if you like) is the secret of deathless living: "This is the bread that comes down from heaven, so that one may eat of it and not die. I am the living bread... the bread that I will give for the life of the world is my flesh." (John 6:50-55).

Questions

1. What does the phrase, "Jesus overcame death," mean to you?

2. What experiences have you had or heard about that convince you or make you question Jesus' statement, "I am the resurrection and the life. Those who believe in me, even thought they die, will live, and everyone who lives and believes in me will never die. " (John 11: 25-26).

3. The gospels record three people being brought back from the dead: Jairus' daughter, the young man from Nain, and Lazarus. What is a timely or an untimely death?

APPENDIX

IS HEALING A CHRISTIAN PRACTICE?

ANSWERS TO QUESTIONS AND CRITICISMS OF DIVINE HEALING

IN MY JOURNEYS all over the country for the purpose of presenting this healing message, it is only natural that I receive many questions and criticisms regarding this work. These questions are easily divided into two types. There are questions which merely ventilate the skepticism of the questioner and there are those which express a genuine desire for knowledge. The first type would be found in the question which asks whether the healing ministry of the New Testament did not close with the gospel age. Such a question usually implies a closed mind. The questioner has already decided that the healing works of the gospel (and the Acts of the Apostles) were granted by God simply to validate the personal ministry of Jesus and his disciples. They believe this age of miracles terminated when the ministry of the twelve apostles terminated and that it would be, therefore, sheer presumption for us to try to continue it. The answer to this question will be found further on in this chapter.

The second type of question comes from those who have a genuine desire for knowledge. Those who ask such questions would like to embrace this healing truth and have a part in its proclamation, but are inhibited by problems for which (thus far) they have found no satisfactory solution. This chapter is an attempt to supply brief answers to those questions.

1. "Is Christian Healing Orthodox Doctrine?

Answer: If the search for health as found and taught in the narratives regarding the healing ministry of Jesus of Nazareth is orthodox Christianity, then the healing ministry which attempts to replicate the kinds of healings that he performed and using his methods are also orthodox. Notice that, as people presented themselves to him for healing, so in modern times this involves a presenting of one's body to God, as the Apostle Paul urged in Romans 12:1:

> I appeal to you therefore, brothers and sisters, by the mercies of God, to present your bodies as a living sacrifice, holy

and acceptable to God, which is your spiritual worship.

Also, it might occur to us logically that if our Lord had to leave the Father's right hand and come down to earth and take human form and live among us in order to accomplish our salvation, surely even the physical life of humankind is important. This is, of course, placing healing on the lowest level, the healing of the human body. But the Apostle Paul further underscores the importance of our bodies by reminding us that they are the temple of the Holy Spirit and therefore deserve special consideration and dedication.

2. ***Is not our salvation more important than our healing?***

   If given a central place in orthodox religion, will not healing usurp the proper place of holiness?

Answer: We do not believe it will. Holiness is the ultimate goal of healthiness. In early English and in other earlier languages, the words *"whole"* and *"holy"* have a common origin. The question fails to comprehend the true meaning of salvation. The very word "salvation" in Latin, Greek, and Anglo-Saxon signifies *wholeness*: to be saved is to *be made whole*. In the New Testament of Wycliffe and Tyndale the words *"health"* and *"salvation"* are used interchangeably, and in the Latin Vulgate the phrase given in the King James Version as *the knowledge of salvation* (Luke 1:77) appears as *scientia salutis* and is rendered by Wycliffe as *science of helthe*.

What the questioner probably intended to ask is, "Is not our salvation more important than our physical well-being?" We would answer 'yes' to this; but salvation implies complete wholeness and the church's ministry of healing today aids men in achieving this complete wholeness. The body is not excluded.

3. *If healing is accepted in the Church, won't the clergy be overworked?*

Answer: The truly consecrated clergy are already overworked. Healing is already accepted in principle in many churches and wise clergy are delegating much of this healing activity to lay assistants and to dedicated prayer groups. Pastoral counseling is another matter and must not be confused with prayer-healing ministrations. A true pastor will realize that even though there may be no time for a scheduled interview, there is always time for prayer.

4. *If the Church practices healing, shall we not attract all sorts of queer people, neurotics, etc.?*

Answer: The Church has always attracted "queer people" as well as more normal folks! Jesus said: "I have not come to call the righteous but sinners to repentance." And again he declared: "Those who are well do not need a physician, but those who are sick!" (Luke 5:31-32). It is estimated that the early Church was recruited largely from those who had been healed, either mentally or physically. Do we want the Church today to operate solely for the benefit of the comfortable and respectable classes? People who find healing in the Church usually prove to be our most convincing publicity.

5. *Does not divine healing tend to make God a "utility"?*

Answer: This question implies that as the Church includes divine healing in its ministry the tendency will be for men to regard God as a "utility" instead of the focus for our highest devotion and worship. It is not our concern to preserve the majesty and honor of God, but rather to obey his commandments as they were given (and are given) through his special agent, Jesus Christ. The command to heal the sick was given in the same breath and correlation as the command to preach the gospel. The salvation of sinners, generally regarded as the essence of the gospel, is not regarded as a "utility," so why should divine healing be so considered? One might equally regard the quest of food as a "utility," yet Jesus encourages us to pray: "Give us this day our daily bread." The danger here is that of undue emphasis on one thing. Recognizing the Almighty as the source of health and the bringer of healing will only add to our devotion and worship, as in the case of David, who exclaimed: "Bless the Lord, O my soul, and all that is within me, bless his holy name… who forgives all your iniquity, who heals all your diseases, who redeems your life from the pit. (Psalm 103:1-2).

6. ***Did not Jesus minimize his healing works? Is it not a fact that while he healed thousands during his first year of public ministry, during the later period he healed few and discouraged those who sought after "signs and wonders"?***

Answer: To make this claim would involve very doubtful exegesis. The four gospels are made of inspired fragments, not chronological history. The principle of divine healing is firmly established by the well-authenticated healing works of Jesus recorded in the gospels and the similar works wrought by his followers in the Acts of the Apostles. Even if it could be established that Jesus wrought fewer miracles during his later ministry, the principle at stake would not be endangered. He had given clear instructions to the twelve (see Luke 9) and to the seventy (see Luke 10) which tied this healing work inexorably with his whole program of redemption and with the affirmation of the present fact of his kingdom. (See Luke 9:2, 10:9.) He affirmed the same connection between healing and the immediacy of the kingdom in his teaching and practice of exorcism – see Luke 11:17-20. That was the standard practice of the Church during the first four centuries, as shown so brilliantly in Dr. Evelyn Frost's book ***Christian Healing***[1] and hence it must still be standard practice and teaching for those who follow the Apostolic tradition today. Wherever the presence of Jesus is felt or affirmed, healing becomes available, whether in the first century or in the twentieth.

---

[1]Frost, Evelyn, ***Christian Healing...In the Light of the Ante-Nicene Church***. London: Mowbray, 1940.

7. *Isn't spiritual healing just a religious use of personal magnetism?*

Answer: This is a very old question and usually circles around some particular individual or local situation. Authorities would not all agree as to precisely what is meant by the words "personal magnetism," but the critics associate it with certain motions of the hands or fingers of the healer while ministering to sick folks, or certain perceptible vibrations felt during the "laying on of hands." We cannot go into the fine points here. Suffice it to say that if the healer possesses some natural gift or talent which speeds up the healing process, we should rejoice and regard it as something coming from above (See James 1:17). The "natural" gifts of physicians, surgeons and physiotherapists are, in a sense, material agencies and roughly placed in the category of "materia medica," yet when these "gifts" are dedicated to God we welcome their use and praise God for the success which follows that use. Why, therefore, should we object to "personal magnetism" if the one who uses it is likewise dedicated? Yet some critics have objected that such powers come from the evil one, just as the religious critics discredited the work of Jesus on similar grounds. (See Luke 11:15, 17-20.) Now, as then, the tree is known by its fruits!

8. ***Isn't divine healing an unwarranted invasion of the field of medical practice?***

Answer: The best answer is that medical doctors do not concur in this criticism. Once we accept the basic principle that "all healing is of God," and that "all healing comes from the Most High" (Sirach 38:1-15) we shall see that ultimately it is the same power which does the work, whether the channel used be that of priest, pastor, evangelist, physician, surgeon, psychotherapist, layworker or intercessor. Each of these, in his own field (and often in friendly collaboration), creates those conditions in which God can work.

9. ***Is there not great danger in the conducting of public healing missions?***

Answer: Yes, there is danger in the conducting of public missions of healing, and there is still greater danger in the neglect or malpractice of such healing evangelism. When we analyze this question and talk privately to the critic who asks the question we find it is provoked usually by (a) prejudice; (b) ignorance of the facts; and (c) some irregularities which have crept into the practice in certain places. The fact that Jesus frequently tied together the proclaiming of his glad tidings, (and the immediacy of his kingdom on earth) with the healing of the sick and the curing of obsessions, is the best of all reasons for holding healing Missions today. Once again we refer the honest critic to Luke 9 and 10, where the instructions given to the Twelve and to the Seventy contemplate a wide audience for this message. The disciples thus commissioned, however, had first received personal instruction from Jesus himself, and later received a special endowment of his Holy Spirit for their work. Our healing evangelism today is clouded and complicated by the obvious defects of those who practice it. Nevertheless, when in honest appraisal is made, we find the arguments strongly in favor of healing missions. The principles and practice of Jesus still work if we give them a chance. The conditions for successful healing evangelism are not too difficult. The simple requirements are: (a) Utter consecration and self-surrender on the part of those who proclaim the public message. (b) Freedom from any profit motive, whether financial or in terms of personal prestige. The evangelist should have had some experience in his own life history of the power of Christ to heal. His attitude will then be summed up in the words: "You have received without payment; give without payment." (c) Preparation of the soil by the local church. Prayer groups should prepare the ground for at least six months before a mission begins. Similar prayer groups should follow up the mission. (d) Local workers should be recruited (largely through the prayer group personnel) to give personal aid to seekers during the mission; the missioner cannot be expected to do much private work during a busy mission. If these conditions are observed, good results will follow, the local churches will be strengthened and a normal or pastoral healing ministry will be established in the locality where the mission is held.

10. Why are so many "good people" not healed after prayer has been offered for them? Doesn't Apostle Paul's thorn in the flesh give the right answer to this question? (See 2 Corinthians 12:7-12.)

Answer: One of the commonest criticisms leveled against divine healing is based upon this passage. It is usually a defense mechanism erected (perhaps subconsciously) by those who fear failure in this work. Many of the best commentators, from St. Chrysostom down to the present day, believe the "thorn" was not any physical disorder in Paul's body, but represented the work of the Enemy, as is implied in verse 7 of the above quotation. The "thorn in the flesh" did not begin with Paul. It is mentioned three times in the Old Testament. (See Numbers 33:55; Joshua 23:13 and Judges 2:3). The reader is urged to study this scriptural data for himself, or at least to read carefully these passages. In every case the "thorn" is the work of the enemy and God's people are urged to keep in right relations with Jehovah in order that they may be preserved or delivered from such enemy action. Since Paul does not reveal the nature of his own "thorn" it seems futile to insist that it must have been a disease or body sickness. Let us grant that it may have been some adverse condition, perhaps even something induced by the apostle's own disposition; the fact remains that he prayed about it and the answer was given: "My grace is sufficient for you; for my power is made perfect in weakness." Weakness need not be pathological; it is primarily lack of strength.

In such conditions the Lord assures his needy disciple that his strength will prove sufficient. For every negative condition we bring to God, he gives us a positive condition to neutralize it. The verse immediately following also justified this attitude: "I am not at all inferior to these super-apostles... You had all the miracles that mark an apostle done for you fully and patiently – miracles, wonders, and deeds of power!" (2 Corinthians 12:11-12). For further comment on this see pamphlet by the Rev. Frank Uttley, of Peterborough, England, *St. Paul's Thorn in the Flesh.*

11. How may I know that the healing for which I pray is God's will?

Answer: Chiefly you may know by your own sincere use of the Lord's Prayer. Jesus said, "Your will be done!" – not "Your will be suffered." The true healing for which we pray (for ourselves) is but a tiny fragment of that larger will of God which Jesus came to make possible. It is significant that we do not find in the gospels any evidence of a sick person coming to Jesus for help and being refused. Never does he argue that the best interest of the seeker – or the larger will of God – will be promoted by the patient remaining in sickness. To our Lord Jesus Christ, as to any good doctor in our own day, disease is an enemy to be vanquished, part of the total result of the accumulated sin of mankind and the work of "The Enemy." If it is the result of sin, the sin must be ventilated and confessed and then Jesus will pour in the balm of absolution: "Son, your sins are forgiven... Rise, take up your bed and walk!" If it is the result of ignorance, then Jesus brings the light of knowledge: "That you may know that the Son of Man has power on earth to forgive sin!" His strength is made perfect in weakness by supplying divine strength to overcome that weakness. If the sickness is the result of inhibitions or obsessions, he casts out the obsessing influence with his inexorable word of command. His Word was with power. It was always the plus sign which canceled out the minus sign of sin and disease. If sickness continued after spiritual ministrations had been given (see Luke 9:37-42; Mark 9:14-29 and Matthew 17:14-21), Jesus diagnosed the lack of faith, or other deficiency, and corrected it, so that God's healing will might be accomplished.

But he never once identified sickness and disease with the will of God. Unfortunately we clergy have (in days gone by) ruined many healing prayers by the safety clause, "if it be your will!" If the patient recovered, then we rejoiced – it was God's will! If the patient died, or remained ill, then we said that was "God's will" and for the ultimate good of all concerned. We were always right! But it was never the teaching and practice of Jesus. Today we are beginning to see the truth on this point! Transition to the next world may well be the "next step" in the pilgrimage of present-day disciples. But there is nothing in holy scripture to indicate that the transition must be brought about by cancer or cerebral palsy or tuberculosis or some other enemy of the race! The will of God in regard to healing is well expressed by the Apostle Peter in his sermon as reported in Acts 10:38: "How God anointed Jesus of Nazareth with the Holy Spirit and with power: who went about doing good and healing all that were oppressed of the devil: for God was with him." Elsewhere we read, "The Son of God was revealed for this purpose, to destroy the works of the devil."

(1 John 3:8). Disease and sickness are certainly among these "works of the devil," even though the sufferer may not himself be the cause of the trouble. When Jesus cured the woman with "a spirit that had crippled her... She was bent over and was quite unable to stand up straight" and had been so afflicted for eighteen years, he declared: "Ought not this woman whom Satan has bound these eighteen years, be set free from this bondage?" (Luke 13:16). We are taught to pray, "Your will be done on earth as it is done in heaven..." That covers every case. We know there is no disease or sin or weakness or misery in heaven. Heaven is that sphere where God's perfect will is always done. Hence our prayer contemplates that what is always done in heaven may now be done here at our point of need. A simple prayer for an emergency treatment would be, "Lord, may your healing will be accomplished in this, your child!" As the prayer is offered, we let go – as far as possible in each case – of all fears, tensions, resentments and unbelief, and feel inwardly that perfect and loving will of God becoming actual in our selves and in those for whom we are praying.

Suppose, after all this, somebody says, "What about our Lord's prayer in Gethsemane, when he said, 'Father, let this cup pass from me; nevertheless, not my will but your will be done!'" We reply: There was no question of disease or sickness involved here. Our Lord was facing the accumulated burden of the world's sin and guilt with vicarious love. The load seemed too great and he almost sank beneath it (see 2 Corinthians 5:21), nevertheless he prayed that the redemptive purpose of his Father might be fulfilled, no matter what the cost to himself. That is unique in all history, the very heart of the Atonement. Let us never presume to identify this unique sacrifice with some local and personal healing prayer.

Questions

1. What is your own answer to people's statement that "the age of miracles" is past and was only for the early church?

2. What seemed to be the purposes of healing by Moses, Elijah, Elisha, Jesus and those in the early church?

3. What is the relationship between healing and believing or having faith in Jesus?

4. The "thorn in the flesh" is referred to also in Numbers 33:55, Joshua 23:13, and Judges 2:3. What does it mean in those places?

   When this is used as a reason for people not being healed, what is Banks' idea?

   What is Jesus attitude toward sickness?